Getting Rich in Real Estate Partnerships

Getting Rich in Real Estate Partnerships

RUTH BAKER BRICKER

WARNER BOOKS

A Warner Communications Company

A Warner/Murray Curtin Book

Warner Books, Inc., 75 Rockefeller Plaza, New York, N.Y. 10019.
A Warner Communications Company

Printed in the United States of America

First printing: February 1982
10 9 8 7 6 5 4 3 2 1

Book design by Judy Allan (The Designing Woman)

Library of Congress Cataloging in Publication Data

Bricker, Ruth Baker, 1930–
Getting rich in real estate partnerships.

Includes index.
1. Real estate investment—Syndication.
I. Title.
HD1382.55.B34 332.63'247 80-29162
ISBN 0-446-51222-2

Dedication

This book is dedicated to Neal S. Bricker,
my husband, the man I've been looking for all my life.

Author's Note

The investment experiences in this book are limited to the Sun Belt. Since real estate laws tend to vary from state to state, and since both real estate laws and tax laws change over time, I would like to stress the need for legal and accounting counsel to anyone considering an investment program.

Contents

Getting Rich in Real Estate Partnerships

Introduction

*T*en years ago, I took a careful look at my financial status. I also projected ahead. The experience brought me to a crossroads in my life.

Using rough figures, I calculated that if I earned $20,000 a year in 1970, I would have to earn over $50,000 a year in 1980 just to keep up with inflation (assuming a rate of 10 percent). But beyond that, in 1990 I would need an annual income of $134,000, and at the time of my retirement (around the year 2000), I would need well over $200,000 a year income just to stay even with my 1970 buying power; or, if my income were to come from investments at a conservative rate of 10 percent, I would need a net worth of $2,000,000 to earn that amount.

It became obvious that I had to find a way out. I needed to increase my net worth enough so that my income could at least keep pace with inflation. Actually what I really wanted was for my standard of living and my spendable income to increase as I grew older.

After an exhaustive search I discovered that real estate values were among the few things that were going up faster than inflation. And so I looked into real estate investment as a solution. For reasons that will become the focal point of this book, I came to the conclusion that *group* investments in real estate offered me the most likely road to financial independence. Although at the time I had limited capital, I owned a piece of property, which I proceeded to sell. The yield, though small, was enough to allow me to launch my new career. The events that have transpired in the last decade have proved that my analysis was correct for the seventies. Will it also be correct for the eighties and the nineties? I believe it will.

Before beginning to describe the "how to" of real estate group investments, I would like to tell you about several events in my earlier life that have shown to be pivotal.

When I was five years old I was in an auto accident and went through the windshield. As a result I spent a good part of my childhood convalescing. My parents were property owners, but because they also were in business, their days were filled, and on a number of occasions they would say to me, "Honey, when you're tired of reading, why don't you try taking care of these ledger books? It will help with your arithmetic." So I began my on-the-job training. Within a short time I was keeping the books, paying the bills, calling the plumber, and reminding the tenants when the rent was overdue. I actually believed that all children did this sort of thing. In fact when other kids asked me what my mother was doing, I'd say, "She's in escrow." By sixteen I was pretty good.

By the age of twenty I had begun to buy small houses, paying $1,000 down, fixing them up, and then selling them for a profit. This of course took place in the fifties and sixties, when it still was possible to buy houses with a minimum downpayment.

When I entered college, my interest in real estate became temporarily sidetracked. I became a student of the arts and sciences. This involvement led to what turned out to be my first career. Some of the projects in the area of arts and sciences that I developed included a laser-light "wall" for the California Institute of Technology, in celebration of the first moon landing; a computer simulation called Trade-Off for California State University at Los Angeles; and, together with almost a hundred artists and scientists in Osaka, Japan, the prototype of the Pepsi-Cola pavilion for Expo '70. The latter was a five-story-high inflatable dome. For the Trade-Off project each participant used a computer terminal to help plan a dream city with a population of 100,000 people. (My master's degree was in urban planning.) The Trade-Off simulation was conducted at an international meeting attended by over 5,000 architects, designers, environmentalists, city planners, ecologists, educators, and students.

My career in the arts and sciences prospered. My activities ultimately came to include the directorship of the publicly funded foundation Experiments in Art and Technology, the editorship of an art journal, invitations to lecture in this country and abroad, etc. But as time passed, I came closer and closer to the realization that my economic survival depended upon monies obtained from government and public institutions, an unstable situation at best. Supported by this awareness, plus the reasons already discussed, I made my decision to reenter the real estate investment field. Thus began my second career.

What I have learned in the last ten years will serve as the basis of the material that I would like to share with you in the pages to follow.

1 Why Real Estate Groups Are Your Best Investment

Nine out of every ten millionaires in the United States made their fortunes investing in real estate. They're staying in real estate, too, because with a real estate investment their money grows, they get an income from the property, and they save on taxes. Where else can you put your money and get all three of those benefits? Not in gold, not in diamonds, not in antiques, not in stocks or bonds or soybean futures.

And more than just United States citizens do well. Look at foreign investors— Iranians, Arabs, Japanese. They know that America is still a great place for property purchases. (It's no secret that some of the biggest property owners in swanky Beverly Hills are foreign investors.)

Foreigners are buying American land as fast as they can; they know the properties they buy will appreciate in value because they are located in a country with a more stable government than most and with a predictably strong economy. Our nation may appear weaker than it once was, but it is still very strong indeed. Income-producing property here is the most sought-after investment in the Western world.

Foreigners know that the phrase "land of the free" isn't just a slogan. People here are mobile, able to move when they want and where they can afford. That encourages the buying and selling of real estate and creates the right climate for making profits.

Change in the 1980s

Real estate was the single best investment during the 1970s. Now we're in a new decade and it's still the right investment for most people, even though the picture has changed dramatically.

There are four major factors affecting real estate as an investment today that make it as attractive as ever:

1. The United States population is growing steadily.
2. There is a shortage of housing.
3. New construction is expensive because the costs of materials, land, loans, and labor are high and keep getting higher.

4. There is a limited amount of usable land—land close to jobs, land that can be farmed.
5. Tax benefits.

First let's look at the increasing population. In the past decade the population of the United States has grown by 30 million people, despite the drop in the number of children per family. There are more elderly people because the average life span is longer now. And we're probably heading into another "baby boom" because the largest group in the country—people in their twenties—are in the family-formation years. More and more Hispanics are entering the United States and they traditionally have large families.

These people and their children and their children's children will need land for housing, land for business and industry, land for commerce, land for recreation, and land for the production of food and fiber. The shortage of housing comes not only from the increase in the number of people but also from the fact that construction isn't keeping up with demand. As demand increases the available supply decreases—and real estate becomes an even more valuable asset.

Builders have to pay extremely high prices for labor and materials, as well as extremely high interest rates for loans, so they're looking for the places they can make the biggest profit—and that isn't in low- or middle-income housing. They're more likely to put up expensive homes or elegant condominiums or large shopping centers.

If you compare today's building costs per square foot to the costs of five to ten years ago, you get a clear picture of why older buildings are gaining in appeal as real estate investments. Not only are supplies for building getting scarcer, they are getting beyond most people's budgets.

On top of that, the cost of filling a car's gas tank is making a lot of people reconsider living in the suburbs. They're looking for homes in the cities, nearer their jobs. That means older mid-city stores are going to be more in demand, too, to serve the returning suburbanites.

There's still a market for the expensive buildings. And older middle-income houses, apartment buildings, and commercial buildings that can be spruced up and qualify for special tax credits can be profitable investments.

A final major plus for real estate investment in the 1980s is the fact that when you buy land, you're not only buying something tangible, you're buying a natural resource that has a limited supply.

Unless we admit another state to the Union, open up federal lands to developers, or, for example, allow the Army Corps of Engineers to double the size of Oakland by filling in part of San Francisco Bay, all the land that will ever exist in the United States exists right now. Land can't be stretched like rubber to meet growing demand, and it can't be manufactured in a factory. All you can do is use it to its maximum.

Land use has its limits, though, because cities regulate building height and impose other zoning restrictions. And unless we want to have people living in rabbit warrens, we shouldn't go beyond a certain population density.

Real estate ownership has always entailed tax benefits. The legislation passed in 1981 has made these benefits even more attractive.

A New Set of Rules

So, undoubtedly, real estate is still a very good place to put your investment money. But today you have to play by almost a whole new set of rules. You need to make a big down payment. Terms of mortgages are likely to be shorter, giving you less time to pay. You'll need a more impressive financial statement to qualify for a loan.

That's why, if you want to break into real estate investment today, your best way is through a real estate group, called a "syndication" in the trade. A syndication is simply a group of people pooling their available cash or other resources to buy, develop, or manage property together.

A group invests in real estate and shares the cost, any income and profits, and the risk. (Yes, just as in any other investment, there is risk. I'll show you how to keep it to a minimum.)

It takes big money to make big money. By joining others in a venture, one average person can have the power of big money. It seems to me that group investing—whatever the property—is the best way to gain the benefits that only wealthy people usually have. By joining a group you have the same clout big investors have, and you can move up the economic ladder to build your income and net worth, as well as reduce the taxes you pay.

A group investment is the key that unlocks the door to the whole world of real estate. It benefits investors at all levels—large, small, or in between.

With $5,000 of yours added to the money put in by

other members of the group, you can buy property worth a great deal more than the total invested because you don't pay the whole purchase price. You pay only a down payment, and you use the lender's money to finance the rest. What you control is worth a good deal more than the down payment—and certainly worth much more than your $5,000 investment.

Overcoming Fear

One of the first things you may experience in considering a real estate group is fear. It is one of the big barriers to making any kind of investment because far too many people let fear hold them back; they may actually end up losing money. You can't even keep up with inflation nowadays by playing it safe with a regular savings account or with money-market investments. To make money you must find an investment that grows faster than inflation.

Ideally, the decision to overcome fear and get started in real estate should be made when you have enough catastrophe protection—health, life, and property insurance—and some savings to tide you over in a financial emergency.

Who Benefits From Group Investments?

Let me tell you about a few of the people I've worked with to illustrate how a real estate group investment helped them reach their goals. A woman I will call Linda had a primary goal: to make a lot of money out of a little money. Her secondary goal was to lower her taxes. Her available investment money was $5,000.

Linda was single, twenty-six, in a middle-management training program in a major corporation. She had an attractive apartment, nice clothes, and a new car—and she paid a lot of income tax each year. Her salary just wasn't going to make her rich; it was enough only to provide for a comfortable life-style.

The only cash that Linda had to invest when she came to me for advice was her savings of $5,000. She asked if she should put the $5,000 into a high-interest certificate of deposit at the bank and wait until she could save enough to invest in real estate on her own.

She had a better alternative, I told her. She could invest with a group. Her $5,000 joined with $5,000 each from nine other people provided the $50,000 needed for a group purchase of a $250,000 apartment building. There were ten partners, each with a one-tenth interest in the building.

Linda became a "limited partner"—she just invested the money and didn't have to watch over the property or get involved in the actual negotiations. Her responsibility and her liability were limited. The one who assumed the liability was the "general partner," who did the legwork of finding the investment property, arranging its purchase, keeping an eye on its management, and ultimately selling it or exchanging it for another property. (I'll discuss these two types of investors—the limited partner and the general partner—in detail later on. And you'll learn how to find a general partner.)

When Linda invested her $5,000 with the group, she signed a partnership agreement that spelled out all the specifics of the real estate group investment. Her money, as well as the funds from the other members of the group, was used for the down payment and closing costs on a six-unit apartment building.

She got one-tenth of the income after expenses and one-tenth of the tax deductions for expenses and depreciation on the property. "Depreciation," a confusing term, refers to a deduction for the *assumed decline* in value caused by aging, even though the property probably increased in value. But for tax purposes depreciation is deductible, as if the value of the building were actually going down.

Rental income from the tenants of the apartment house was used to make monthly mortgage payments and tax payments, and to meet all the other costs of operating the building. Linda deducted her one-tenth of expenses and depreciation from her taxable income.

These tax deductions, then, are the first major benefit of a properly structured group real estate investment. But there are others.

Linda got one-tenth of the money left over after the expenses of operating the apartment building were paid. She earned 6 percent on her original $5,000 investment in the first year. That's the second benefit of a well-managed group real estate investment: income.

As the mortgage payments are made the balance due on the mortgage is reduced. At the same time, this particular building was actually gaining in value because the demand for this type of income-producing property was growing and the general value of all real estate in the area was rising. (The increased value—the increase in amount a buyer would be willing to pay for it—is called "appreciation.")

Together, the reduction of the mortgage and the increase in value meant the investors' equity was growing. "Equity" is the market value of a property after deducting the balance due on the mortgage, and "market value" is the amount a buyer would be willing to pay to purchase the property. Increased equity is the third benefit of a well-run group investment.

There is still another major benefit. Linda's original $5,000 investment remains intact. She will recover it—and considerably more—as soon as the apartment house is sold or when it is exchanged (if an even better investment comes along).

As a limited partner Linda is able to have her money working for her, but she doesn't have to devote time and energy to the investment. If she stays in well-run group investments and reinvests her profits, she'll be on her way to her goal. She'll be able to build the fortune she seeks and at the same time will have deductions to shelter her from income taxes.

Linda's story—the benefits she got and will continue to get from putting her money into a group real estate venture—is the model for all such investments. There are individual circumstances and differences, but basically the benefits remain the same.

A carefully designed and well-managed group real estate investment can, then, provide these advantages:

1. A shelter from taxes.
2. An increasing equity over and above original investment.
3. Spendable return from the rental income.

The story of Harold and Dorothy is different. Their primary goal was to shelter their high salaries from income taxes. Their secondary goal was to develop a source of income for retirement. Their available investment money was $100,000.

Harold is a thirty-eight-year-old accountant. His wife, Dorothy, is a thirty-seven-year-old school administrator. He makes $62,500 a year from his accounting firm, and Dorothy's gross income is more than $28,000. They're in a high income-tax bracket.

They had $50,000 saved, with most of it in certificates of deposit. They got a fixed return—that is, a set amount of interest on the principal—but the principal itself didn't grow in value.

Harold and Dorothy lived in a large house with a low mortgage. The house was worth $210,000 when they sought my advice. They could raise $50,000 by borrowing against their house through a second trust deed, which would provide more investment funds and more tax deductions (from the interest on that loan).

Over the years, Harold had told his clients how to lower their taxes, but he hadn't done much about lowering his own. He finally decided to take some of his own advice and seek a tax shelter for himself and Dorothy.

Harold and Dorothy were conservative. They wanted to spread their investments to spread their risk. They cashed in their certificates of deposit and put that $50,000 into one real estate group investment—the purchase of a middle-income apartment complex. Their $50,000 bought them a 10 percent interest as limited partners.

Using some simple guidelines—the kind you'll find later in this book—Harold expected that the sale of this apartment complex in two or three years would bring $250,000 in profit on the original investment of

$500,000 ($50,000 each from ten partners). Harold and Dorothy would get one-tenth of that $250,000 anticipated profit—$25,000—plus a return of the original investment of $50,000 when the building was sold. They planned to keep reinvesting the money, which would provide an increasingly large tax shelter as their investment grew.

Harold learned that the owner of the office building in which his firm is located planned to sell the building through a different kind of group investment—office condominiums. With the $50,000 from the second loan on his house he had enough for a down payment on his office suite. The total price was $350,000.

The condominium association's monthly maintenance fees were lower than his rental payment had been, and as an owner he gets full benefit of tax write-offs just as he had with rent. The difference is that now his money is *earning* money. The condominium will increase in value. He doesn't have to worry about rent increases. And when he's ready to retire, the suite can be sold and the money used for retirement income.

For some people a combination of real estate and other investments is wise, as in the case of Agnes, a sixty-one-year-old widow, who received a sizable amount of insurance money when her husband died. She had to use the money to support herself, since it was her only source of income.

To set up an established monthly income to meet her living expenses, Agnes put half her money into certificates of deposit and second trust deeds. To assure herself of funds and a nest egg for the years ahead, she invested the other half of the funds in the group purchase of a shopping center that had good growth potential. Agnes' investments must support her for perhaps twenty to thirty years, and this combination—fixed income plus real estate—should do the job well.

Sometimes an investor has some money that he or she can afford to take more risks with than a person like Agnes can. Sam, who left his corporate job at forty-three to become a self-employed businessman is an example. His business did very well, so when he got the $15,000 from his former employer's pension plan it was the kind of extra money he was able to invest with some degree of risk. He didn't want to lose it, of course, but he could wait to get his profit later. And he wanted to do something different with it.

Sam used the $15,000 to become part-owner of an industrial warehouse in a deteriorated part of town. He and his partners converted the warehouse into a self-storage building. Sam did some of the conversion work himself, earning an additional percentage of the deal by using his labor instead of cash.

The partners can sell the self-storage business and keep the building, or they can sell the building and keep the business, or they can sell both. But they are willing to wait for a revitalization of their inner-city location. It could take many years, but in the meantime the property is earning enough to pay for itself. Someday they hope to convert the building into office suites or a wholesale shopping center.

Your own goals and your own story may be similar to one or more of these examples. Or perhaps your situation involves still another set of circumstances.

Whatever your interests, whatever your goals and objectives, real estate group investment probably will help you take the first step toward the goal of financial security.

To see if group investing is for you, if it will meet your needs, and if you are the kind of person who can benefit from group investing, answer the following questions:

- Can you get cash or its equivalent to put into an investment? (The equivalent might be certain financial paper that is accepted in place of cash.)
- Do high real estate costs and high mortgage rates keep you away from real estate investments?
- Are you willing to conquer some of the fear you may have—as we all do—about investing, and not let it hold you back?
- Are you willing to be patient, to set your sights on a not-too-distant success story instead of choosing quick profits?
- Are you willing to put in some time to study the subject and to become familiar with your own needs and goals?
- Are you willing to accept the possibility that there are risks in any investment?

If you answered yes to these questions, you're a good candidate for group investing in real estate. But you're going to have to put some effort into getting to know about group investing and how to be a success at it.

That's what this book is all about. It is a workbook that explains group investing: what it is and what it isn't; its benefits and risks; what it takes in time, money, and knowledge; how to make it work for you.

You'll become familiar with the language of real estate and group investing, and you'll learn what to expect.

In later chapters I'll show you how to invest wisely and confidently. I'll review the roles of the general partner and the limited partner. I'll explain the difference between public and private offerings. I'll talk about different types of property and how to tell a good piece of property from a lemon. You'll read about financing, buying, selling, and exchanging property.

There's a lot to learn, but it's worth the effort. Just keep remembering those millionaires who made their fortunes in real estate. It may not be as easy to do today, but it's still possible—especially if you invest with a group.

If you're *still* wondering if investing in group real estate is a wise move, ask yourself these further questions:

- At any time in the last ten years have you invested in stock and lost money?
- Have you invested in real estate in the last ten years and lost money?

Try asking a lot of other people these questions, too. When you tally the answers, you'll find the situation is lopsided. People who invested in stocks and bonds lost money sometime during the last decade. Far fewer, lost money in real estate investments.

So come along and find out the rest of what you need to know to be a wise investor in real estate groups. Next you're going to get a chance to evaluate your own goals and see just how much money you have available for an investment.

2 Designing Your Financial Future

Whatever your goals are—travel, a college education for your children, a mountain cabin, a larger house, a boat, enough cash to change careers—they *can* be reached. Investing in real estate with a group can make it all happen, and there's no secret formula. The process is based on the economic facts of life.

If you want true financial strength and financial security, you need to take action for yourself. No employer or government agency can be counted on to provide it. Too many people have discovered that for themselves. Ask anyone who is trying to live now on retirement income geared to the economy of a low-inflation era. The pension and Social Security checks just don't stretch to fit today's cost of necessities.

If you want to plan your own security and decide where you want to be in the future, the first step is to see where you are *today* by checking out your net worth. You'll want to know how much you can invest now and what you'll need to do to get the money for future investments.

In conducting seminars in real estate investing in this country and abroad, I've learned that most people don't really know how much they're worth in dollars and cents. So one of the first things to do before you take your nest egg out of the bank and put it into a group investment is to check yourself out financially, using the questions below:

- Do you own your own home?
- Have you ever had a tax shelter?
- Have you ever invested in real estate other than your own home?
- Have you ever participated in a real estate group investment?
- Have you ever managed real estate other than your own home?
- Have you established credit in your own name?
- Have you ever filled out a financial statement?
- Have you ever qualified for a real estate loan in your own name?
- Is the bulk of your savings kept in long-term certificates of deposit?
- Do you pay a substantial portion of your income every year in income taxes?

The answers to these questions indicate where you need to add to your real estate knowledge. A "yes" answer to the first eight questions shows you already have some firsthand experience that will be useful to you as a group investor. A "yes" answer to the last two questions illustrates how you can benefit from group investments in real estate by making your money do a better job for you.

A lot of people become paralyzed by indecision just because they don't have "yes" answers to the first eight questions. They put all their extra cash into low-paying savings accounts because they are unsure about what to do with it, and they miss all the better opportunities because of this lack of knowledge.

You'll need a financial statement if you get into a group investment, just as a financial statement is necessary to open a new business. Group investment, after all, *is* a business. You'll probably need a financial statement for borrowing the money to be invested and again when the actual investment is made. And it just might please you to find out how high your net worth is. Many people are pleasantly surprised and find that the effort of compiling a financial statement is worthwhile for that reason alone.

To demonstrate how a statement looks, we will follow the process with a couple who are considering group real estate investments. Paul and Carol filled out the following form, which indicated what their holdings are right now and gave an idea of what they might be able to borrow for investment capital. (There's a blank form for your own use on pp. 29–32

FINANCIAL STATEMENT
(inventory of assets and liabilities)

ASSETS (what you own)

CURRENT ASSETS (easily turned into cash)

Cash on hand	$ 204
Cash in checking account	1,803
Cash in savings account	6,108
Cash in short-term certificates of deposit (CDs)	10,000
Accounts receivable—current	——
Notes receivable—current	——
Stocks and bonds	14,330
Other current assets (describe)	——
Total current assets	$32,445

FIXED ASSETS (can't be turned into cash immediately; use current market value, not original cost)

Notes secured by deeds, mortgages, or other real estate liens	$ ——
Accounts and notes receivable	——
Due from relatives	420
	——
Real estate (residence)	117,890
Cash value of life insurance	4,455
Automobiles	7,830
Other assets (describe)	
Retirement fund	18,400
Home furnishings	8,400
Personal effects (coin collection, jewelry, etc.)	1,790
Camera equipment	810
Total Assets	$192,440

LIABILITIES (what you owe)

Current liabilities	
(debts due in less than a year)	
Note payable to bank	$ ——
Other notes payable, due within one year	——
Accounts and bills payable—not due	3,230
Accounts and bills payable—past due	——
Due to relatives	——
Mortgages	53,385
due within a year	——
Notes secured by personal property	——
Other current liabilities (describe)	
Pledge to charity	760
Income taxes due	——
Total Liabilities	$62,375

NET WORTH (total assets minus total liabilities: what you are worth after all your debts are subtracted from the value of all you own)	$130,065

Paul and Carol hadn't realized just how much they were worth. They knew they had the cash and savings and their equity in the real estate but hadn't stopped to think of the value of their insurance and retirement fund and some of their other, less obvious assets. They could use this statement in applying for a bank loan and for establishing their ability to invest in a group real estate purchase.

Now try it for yourself:

YOUR FINANCIAL STATEMENT
(inventory of assets and liabilities)

ASSETS

CURRENT ASSETS

Cash on hand	$
Cash in checking account	
Cash in savings account	
Cash in short-term certificates of deposit	
Accounts receivable—current	
Notes receivable—current	
Stocks and bonds listed on exchanges	
Other current assets (describe:)	______
Total current assets	$

FIXED ASSETS

Notes secured by deeds, mortgages, or other real estate liens	$
Accounts and notes receivable	
Due from relatives	
Stocks and bonds	

Real estate (residence)
Real estate (other)
Cash value of life insurance
Automobiles
Other assets (describe:) ______
Total assets

LIABILITIES

Current Liabilities

Notes payable to bank	$
Other notes payable, due within one year	
Accounts and bills payable—not due	
Accounts and bills payable—past due	
Due to relatives	
Mortgages due within a year	
Notes secured by personal property	
Other current liabilities (describe:)	
Income taxes due	______
Total current liabilities	$

Other Liabilities

Mortgages, trust deeds, other real estate liens due after a year	$
Notes and bills payable, due after a year	
Other liabilities (describe:)	______
Total Liabilities	$______

NET WORTH (assets minus liabilities) $______

For your records, you also may want to list the following:

Insurance: type, amount, company, and beneficiary.
Stocks and bonds: number of shares, description of item, to whom issued, cost, market value today.
Real estate: address, in whose name it is held, cost, market value today, unpaid balance, monthly payments, name of mortgage holder.

Now you know your net worth. The next critical question is, How much money can you invest in a group real estate purchase?

Paul and Carol came up with the following facts and figures:

INVESTMENT CAPITAL

OCCUPATIONAL INCOME

Husband's annual income (including bonuses and commissions, before taxes and other deductions)	$36,000
Wife's annual income (including bonuses and commissions, before taxes and other deductions)	19,500
Other occupational income (part-time or second job, etc.)	2,400
Total	$57,900
Amount (after taxes, other deductions, and cost-of-living expenses) that can be set aside for investment this year	$10,422

OTHER INCOME	
Interest income	$ 1,853
Stock dividends	1,218
Annuities	——
Real estate income	——
Tax-refund estimate	——
Total	$ 3,071
Amount that can be set aside for investment this year	$ 3,071

ASSETS THAT CAN BE TURNED INTO CASH	
Life insurance (cash value)	$ 4,455
Savings	17,000
Additional cash that will be available when current liabilities are paid (cash available in the next six months)	1,400
Personal line of credit (how much you can borrow from the bank on your signature alone)	5,000
Savings bonds	——
Other cash assets	300
TOTAL	$28,155
Amount that can be set aside for investment this year	$28,155

REAL ESTATE EQUITY	
Market value of residence	$117,890
Minus mortgage or other loans	– 58,385
Equity in home	$59,505
Other property (market value)	$ ——
Minus mortgage or other loans	– ____
Equity in other property	——
Total (equity in real estate)	$59,505
Amount you would be willing to use as collateral for a second mortgage (after considering cost of borrowing funds and payments required to pay it back, minus amount you save because you have an additional tax deduction for interest payments)	$19,055

SUMMARY OF INVESTMENT CAPITAL	
Occupational income	$10,422
Other income	3,071
Assets	28,155
Real estate equity loan	19,055
Total (investment capital available)	$60,703

Paul and Carol have decided they can reasonably gather a little more than $60,000 for a group investment. Some of the computations were fairly simple—the amount of assets and other income, for example. But when it came to figuring out how much they could save from their joint incomes, they had to make some serious decisions.

Paul and Carol don't have children now, although they're considering starting a family in a few years. They've been spending most of their disposable income on weekends in the Bahamas. Also, several evenings a week they dine at fine restaurants.

Paul and Carol conclude that they won't be happy changing their life-style drastically—at least not until they've started a family—but there are definitely ways to cut back. Doing without some of the pleasures today can mean a better economic life in the future. They'll reduce their entertainment budget by one-third and use that money for investing.

The other part of their investment-capital survey that took special thought was whether or not they wanted to get a second mortgage on their home. After comparing the advantages of each, they decided a moderate second-trust-deed loan was reasonable. The interest rate was higher than they liked, but there was an advantage. They could recapture a large part of the interest payment because it is tax deductible.

They'll also be looking for a group investment that gives them a good tax shelter. The more money they can keep (instead of paying it out in income taxes), the more money they will have to invest.

What about your own investment potential? Complete this survey and you'll have that answer:

YOUR INVESTMENT CAPITAL

OCCUPATIONAL INCOME

Your annual income (including bonuses and commissions, before taxes and other deductions) $

Your spouse's annual income, (including bonuses and commissions, before taxes and other deductions)

Other income (part-time or second job, etc.) ______

TOTAL

Amount (after taxes, other deductions, and living expenses) that you can set aside for investments this year $

OTHER INCOME

Interest income $

Stock dividends

Annuities

Real estate income

Tax-refund estimate ______

TOTAL $

Amount you can set aside for investment this year $

ASSETS THAT CAN BE TURNED INTO CASH

Life insurance (cash value) $

Savings

Additional cash that will be available when current liabilities are paid (cash available in the next six months)

Personal line of credit (how much you can borrow from the bank on your signature alone)		
Savings bonds		
Other cash assets		______
TOTAL		$
Amount you can set aside for investment this year		$

REAL ESTATE EQUITY

Market value of residence	$	
Minus mortgage or other loans	– ______	
Equity in home		$
Other property (market value)	$	
Minus mortgage or other loans	– ______	
Equity in other property		______
Total (equity in real estate)		$
Amount you would be willing to borrow for a second mortgage (after considering cost of borrowing funds and the payments required to pay it back, minus amount you save because additional tax deductions for interest payments)	$	

Now total all these figures to arrive at the amount of investment capital you can put into a real estate group:

Summary of Your Investment Capital

Occupational Income	$
Other income	$
Assets	$
Real estate equity loans	$______
Total (investment capital available)	$______

Identify Your Investment Goals

Before you actually use that investment capital to get into a group, you need to ask yourself more questions:

- Are you interested primarily in saving income taxes? That is, could you afford to invest in something that yields no income for a while, provided it lowers your income-tax payments?
- Is your aim a second income to supplement your present salary or retirement income?
- Are you planning for a specific future goal, such as money for your children's college education, for your own retirement, or for a second home?

Your goal will determine the best type of investment for you. You should select an investment with goals that match your own.

Another decision you must make is the role you will take in the group, once you know how to find one: If you want to make the investment and get the advantages without full-time involvement, you will participate as a limited partner. If you want to be in charge—put the project together, make the decisions, and accept the demands on your time—you will be the general partner.

The next two chapters deal with what a general partner does, how to find one, and how to be one.

3 What a General Partner Does

Let's assume that you are going to be a limited partner. The great advantage is that even though you don't—and can't—actively take part in the buying, managing, and selling of a property, a pro-rata (proportionately determined) share of the income goes to you. And you can deduct expenses from your income tax to the extent of your percentage of participation, and your loss, if any, is limited to the amount stated in your partnership agreement. You get all the benefits without having to deal with all the time-consuming details.

It is the general partner who puts together the group investment and nurses it along, so you must be sure to choose a well-qualified man or woman. They come in all types—competent and incompetent, hardworking and lazy, honest and dishonest. You need to understand the role of a general partner before you start searching for one.

The legal definition of a real estate group investment with respect to syndicators is "an association of two or more persons, for profit, where the Investor relies on the efforts of the Manager [General Partner] to maintain the invested capital."* There are specific tasks that the general partner handles in that role.

The General Partner's Tasks

First he must locate the investment property, which is not an easy task. In addition to researching the physical characteristics of the property, the general partner must study the investment aspects—its operating expenses, income, and financial potential. Written proposals (called "setups") are seldom clear-cut. He has to discover what they really mean by making phone calls (to owners, managers, and real estate brokers), visiting sites, and checking everything carefully.

The second task is to acquire the property. At that time the general partner must negotiate with the seller to get the best price—and, most important, the best possible financing.

My method is to use my own money for the down payment and then write a contract that allows me time to bring in limited partners. (Of course, the contract is

*Ronald A. Anderson and Walter A. Kumpf, *Business Law* (Cincinnati: South-Western Publishing Company, 1972)

drawn up with the help of my attorney. Unless you're careful, you could lose the down payment.)

Sometimes general partners will buy the property themselves, then sell it to the limited partners. They get all their profit out of the transaction at the front end rather than take it later, when the limited partners do. Although I prefer a group investment in which the general and limited partners buy—and profit—at the same time, your particular investment goals may make the profit-later arrangement acceptable.

The third task for the general partner is to form a group in which each member understands exactly what the goals are: what tax advantages are being offered, how profits will be distributed, the likely profit potential, and the risk.

These conditions should be spelled out in the agreement that is signed by the general partners and the limited partners. Obviously, the agreement can't promise a definite profit, sale price, operating expense, or income. These are variables that depend in part on the skills of the general partners and in part on such outside factors as the state of the economy, and supply and demand.

The written agreement should state general goals. For example, it might say that the purpose of the investment is to produce maximum monthly income or that the investment is not expected to produce any income for the first two years. Whatever the goal is, it should be stated in writing.

And the limited partner—you—should be sure to understand the agreement completely. If you don't, ask questions and consult with your attorney and accountant.

Fourth on the list of general-partner tasks is coping with all the paperwork necessary for buying, maintaining, and selling the property. If you've ever bought real estate, you know that even the simplest deal involves a lot of red tape—and even more in a group investment. This task is an important one.

The purchasing of property often calls for four documents: the offering memorandum about the investment, the participation agreement, the limited-partnership agreement, and the certificate of limited partnership. They are all legal documents that require the assistance of the general partner's attorney and accountant. Together they must determine the best kind of legal framework for the group investment. (I'll talk more about these documents in Chapter 9.)

Task number five is managing the property when it's owned by the group. Often the general manager will have a property manager at the site or at a number of his sites. But the general manager must have real expertise. There are some critical ongoing decisions that have to be made, and many of them affect your investment. It's important to have a general partner who knows when to make repairs and when to delay them, when to raise rents and how to do it legally in a rent-control area, how to handle difficult tenants, how to maintain the property efficiently, how to hire and fire employees, and how to manage managers.

Remember that under the Internal Revenue Code a group investment is an *investment.* This means you bought the property as an investment, not for the purpose of reselling it or exchanging it. A general partner who knows how to manage the property—to keep it in good operating condition without frivolous spending—is essential.

The time will come, no doubt, when the best course is to sell or exchange the property. Determining that time is the sixth task of the general partner. Sometimes you'll do best if you hold on to the property for spendable income. At other times you can use it to trade up to a better property with bigger profit.

But making the decision to sell or exchange is only the first step. The general partner also needs to determine how it will be marketed—it might be sold or exchanged—and what financing will be offered.

The decision to sell or hold or exchange a property can mean the difference between making a profit and having your money tied up for years in an investment. For example, in one small group the general partner decided to sell. There were three limited partners, each of whom had invested $15,000. When the building was sold, they had to carry back a sizable second trust deed; that is, they had to handle the financing for the buyer rather than have a bank or savings-and-loan association do it. The paper profit on the sale was $120,000, but they got only $30,000 in cash—$10,000 for each of the three investors. The rest was due on a five-year second trust deed. They probably could have done better if they had held the property until the market stabilized or until they could get a buyer with a larger down payment.

The seventh task of the general partner is the overriding one: to return the investment capital plus a reasonable profit. If you, the limited partner, don't want to make more money that year, you can reinvest it. Sometimes you'll reinvest with the same goals; sometimes you'll need to find a different group because your goals have changed.

What a General Partner Does:

1. Locates and checks out the investment.
2. Acquires the property by contract so it can be bought by the group or acquires it and then sells it to the group.
3. Forms the group with a clearly stated investment goal.
4. Handles the paperwork, starting with the offering memorandum, the participation agreement, the limited-partnership agreement, and the certificate of limited partnership.
5. Manages the property during the time it's held by the group.
6. Determines the best time to sell or exchange the property.
7. Reaches the stated goal, returning investment capital plus profit.

Payments to the General Partner

A general partner is paid in three ways: fees, commissions, and earnings.

A fee is paid for packaging the group investment, which includes all the details of setting up the deal, and can range from 10 percent to 80 percent of the profits from the property. The average is about 50 percent. This fee is commonly paid when the property is sold. From cash remaining after all expenses of the sale, the limited partners' initial investment capital is returned. The balance is divided among the general partners and limited partners according to the percentages agreed on at the beginning.

Some general partners take their fee at the beginning, out of the investors' contributions. If this is done, I think the fee should be no more than 10 percent. I am wary about up-front payments, for there is no advantage to the limited partner. I believe, rather, that the general partner should take his chances along with the limited partners.

Commissions or finder's fees may be paid to a general partner on the purchase of the property as well as on the sale.

Earnings from the property are a third source of payment to the general partner, who will often take part of the spendable income on a pro-rata basis. That is, if he has a 10 percent investment in the property, he will get 10 percent of the income after expenses, as well as 10 percent of the tax deduction for those expenses.

To summarize, the general partner can be compensated for the following:

- Putting the deal together.
- Managing the partnership and overseeing property management.
- Personally managing the property.
- Earning a broker's commission for both the purchase and the sale of the property.
- Investing in the property along with the other partners. (He or she gets a percentage of profit after returning the capital-investment contributions to the limited partners.)

Being a General Partner—Possible Drawbacks

Let's assume now that *you* want to take on the job of being a general partner. There are specific precautions I want to mention. You should know it is a time-consuming, money-consuming job if you want to do it right. And I speak from personal experience with all the problems.

There are expenses before you'll ever see a dime of profit for your efforts. You may have to travel extensively to find the "right property" (which I will describe in Chapter 6). I have looked at offers on as many as *five hundred* properties before finding something worthwhile. And after I find a property that looks attractive on paper, there are trips to the city planning department, to local attorneys and brokers, and to neighboring properties. Not only is my time being eaten up; there are also hotel bills and meals and transportation. While I'm traveling my mortgage still comes due back home. So do other bills. There's no "boss" to pick up the tabs. As a general partner you're your own boss when it comes to paying bills.

You'll also need earnest money when you find a suitable property, and you'll sometimes have to have down-payment money yourself if you want to take advantage of an immediate opportunity to get a good price on the right property—even before you've put the group together.

Once you've picked the property, your key job as a general partner is to find the limited partners to join in the investment. You are responsible for other people's money—sometimes the bulk of their life savings. If you lose, they lose. You can't be casual about that responsibility. It's a heavy burden, one that's acceptable only if you have reason to feel confident in your own knowledge and expertise.

General partners also have to be patient. Good group investments usually take time. It can easily take three to six months to find a suitable property. Then there is additional time for negotiations, making an offer, and making an inspection. These can consume at least two weeks. Then you have to meet with your experts to prepare the contract, the offering memorandum, and the limited-partnership agreement (all of which I'll tell you about). That can take another month. Next you have to raise the money and get all the partners in agreement—finding people who have the same investment goals you do, taking time to explain things to many people so that some, the right ones, come aboard as limited partners. Here, again, a month or two is common.

Even after you buy the property for the group, there's a time requirement. You'll need to manage the property or oversee its management for a year or two or more. The last step, selling or exchanging, takes time, too—time to find a buyer, time to negotiate.

A general partner must make some commitments—commitments of time, money, and energy. You'll need to understand all the different kinds of properties, how to handle them in changing market conditions, and how to cope with the unpredictable.

As a general partner you will have to face the sometimes awkward experience of asking friends for money. Those friends and their friends are your investors. Once you have a track record of some success, you'll probably have potential investors coming to you. But at first you have to do the asking.

If you are willing to face all the responsibilities and accept all the risks, being a general partner can be rewarding. For most people, however, limited partnership is a more realistic role.

4 What to Look for in a General Partner

The ideal general partner seems to be a combination of saint, paragon, and miracle-worker—a hero out of fiction. But top-flight general partners *do* exist. There *are* men and women who have all or most of the characteristics needed. But just where do you find this wizard who takes your money, keeps you happy, and achieves the outcome of a cash profit?

If you don't want to be a general partner, the best way to start finding one is by asking people who have already made group investments, say, for example, your doctor, a reliable real estate broker, or an accountant or lawyer you respect. You can get their opinions and recommendations, but of course you must do your own sleuthing to be sure that the general partner they praise so highly is the right kind for you.

I recommend that you look for someone with characteristics close to your own—not the same, but similar. I suggest you find someone who is near you in age, educational background, and economic status. It should be someone who lives near you and understands your life-style—And, most important, someone with similar investment goals. Then, if the times get rough, you have that common background and understanding of each other that can help solve or minimize problems. Most of the investors I work with are friends of people who have been referred to me by friends or previous investors.

Once you've found a general partner who has the desired characteristics, you should check further so that you can decide whether to invest with him or her or to wait until you find someone more appropriate. (I usually use the singular, "general partner," but it is just as likely that you'll be dealing with several general partners in a group investment.)

Dig Beneath the Surface

Warning: Don't be charmed by surface appearances.

There is, for example, the case of my friend Jim, who put all his investment capital into a group because he was so impressed with what the three general partners had to say about themselves, the property, and the great profit opportunity. Jim visited their plush offices. The furniture radiated the message that these people were highly successful.

Jim's partnership with this trio became rocky, however, when he discovered that the great profit they had talked about was *their* profit—taken at the beginning out of the limited partners' money (including Jim's). The limited partners had to wait until the sale of the property to get any substantial benefit from the investment.

The other investors had understood the arrangement and were willing to go along with it, even though they might have done better if they had checked further. Jim was in a dilemma because he had counted on spending income from the investment. He had to live with the fact that he was at fault for having accepted the deal. He hadn't taken the necessary steps or asked the necessary questions to assure himself that he and the general partners could live harmoniously in their partnership.

He had fallen for their charm and deep carpeting, and then found himself in a relationship that he didn't like. Pulling out of the group early would have meant a loss instead of a profit, so Jim had to rearrange his finances and stay with this unsatisfactory situation until the property was sold and he could get his money—and profit—out. The next time, he did his homework before making a group investment.

A Dozen "Deciders"

When you want to evaluate a potential general partner, you can use the checklist below. If there is more than one general partner, you should be sure that *collectively* they bring to the transaction all the qualities and characteristics that are important to assure success for your investment. If your potential general partner (or partners) is to pass this test, he or she

- Has a successful investment history.
- Has demonstrated negotiating skills.
- Knows how to evaluate property—when and how to buy property to match the goals of the investors.
- Has a team of skilled, reliable certified public accountants and attorneys who specialize in real estate.
- Supplies you with a list of names, addresses, and telephone numbers of people who have recently invested with him or her.
- Has a strong financial statement, a good credit rating, and an excellent relationship with a bank.
- Makes modest promises about what he or she can do for you through a group investment and can back up these promises with facts and figures.
- Understands financial planning and city planning.
- Gives you a clear explanation of fees, commissions, and his or her participation in the group investment.
- Is skilled at property management and record keeping.
- Is willing and able to invest his or her own money in the group investment.
- Is guided by all the rules that apply to public offerings.

If your prospective general partner has a similar background to yours *and* does well on the checklist, then you have found a gem and you ought to move to the next step, discussing the specific transaction.

Sometimes a general partner won't do well on one or more points. The importance of such shortcomings depends on just where he or she is weak.

Investment Experience

If someone you've known well for a long time—someone you are sure is capable and has done well in business—decides to be a general partner for the first time, then you may not be overly concerned that he doesn't have a history of successful real estate investments. He should still score high in other areas, however, such as financial standing and know-how. He should have good, knowledgeable people to assist him when unfamiliar problems and concerns arise. There are some points, however, that are particularly important for *all* general partners, new or experienced.

Keep in mind that a successful investment history is especially important if you don't know the general partner well. Of course, everyone has to start somewhere. Limited partners have to use their own judgment when starting with someone new.

Negotiating Skills

This second point in the checklist is an important one. Those skills don't necessarily have to be demonstrated in real estate purchases, but that kind of experience—including individual purchases as well as group investments—is valuable. The general partner is going to need to know when to stand fast in negotiations and not be pushed into a deal.

Sellers can be unreasonable and unmovable. If a general partner has good negotiating skills, he can cope with that inflexibility and find another way to achieve a mutually satisfactory agreement. Perhaps the seller won't move an inch on price but is willing to handle the financing in a way that is attractive and beneficial to the group. It's up to the general partner to find that solution.

Good negotiating skills lead to good transactions. If a prospective general partner doesn't have these skills, it can cost you money and keep you away from profit-making investments.

Evaluating Property

The skills involved here can be learned. So what you need more than anything else is someone who understands the key points about what makes a property valuable, as well as how and when to buy it. Then that understanding has to be translated into action. You can evaluate a potential general partner's ability by reading about how to make a good property out of a potential lemon (see Chapter 6) and then listening to what he or she has to say about a philosophy of selecting investment property.

Be Backed by a Team

This backup is essential. Any general partner worth your trust will have a team of experts who can supply professional counsel. Sometimes the general partner is also an attorney or a CPA and doesn't feel any help is needed. But unless he is an expert in *real estate* taxes and accounting, don't be satisfied. His knowledge has to be specific: real estate. A skilled attorney or CPA can lead your group to increased tax benefits, as well as put the brakes on potential problems—in the contract as well as in operations and management later.

If the investment is out of state, then two teams of experts are needed, an attorney and accountant in the general partner's home state and another team in the state where the property is located. It's even better if the attorneys and accountants practice in the *cities* where the general partner and the investment property are. Each state and city has its own laws regarding property. You can save yourself a great deal of psychological and financial distress if you know you are protected by skilled, well-regarded counselors.

References

You will want to get references—at least four or five—from the prospective general partner. The list should include people who are currently limited partners with this general partner and people who have recently been limited partners.

It's not necessary to get into the personal aspects of the financial transaction between the general partner and the references. You can get a great deal of information from basic questions that never address the questions of how much money was invested and how much profit was made, which some people might be unwilling to tell you.

Below is a list of questions you should ask:

- How did you hear about this general partner?
- Are you now in a partnership with him?
- If not, when did you last do business together?
- What kind of property was involved?
- What was the goal of the investment, and was it met?
- Did you get the results promised at the beginning of the transaction?
- Is this general partner also a licensed real estate broker?
- If so, do you believe any of his decisions were influenced by his desire to get a sales commission?
- Have you recommended him to any of your friends or family, and if not, why not?
- Did the general partner keep you up-to-date at least every three months on what was happening with the investment?
- Is the general partner accessible by phone or in person when you have a question?
- Would you invest with him again?

Obviously, if your general partner has no investment history, there can't be a list of past investor references. That's one reason it's wise to go with someone experienced if you don't know him well.

Financial Statement, Credit Rating, Bank Relationship

It is essential that your prospective general partner—in fact, each general partner if there is more than one—has a strong financial statement, a good credit rating, and an excellent relationship with a bank.

The general partner assumes liability for the investment. If there is an emergency or some other problem—a recession, a cutback, an unusually long heat wave—you must be sure the general partner has the financial stability to tide him over during the crisis, to keep the property intact without having to go to you and the other limited partners for money. This financial stability, including a good banking relationship, is your protection against calamity.

Partnership agreements often provide that the limited partners can be requested to invest more money. You need the assurance that if this request is made and you are unable to chip in, the contract provides a way for you to sell or reduce your equity in the property.

In some cases the general partner can bring in additional limited partners, thus diluting the group. Whether you are a limited or general partner, you must know in advance if this is a possibility.

Phony Promises

No general partner, experienced person or beginner, should promise more than he or she can deliver. A modest investment package is more likely to be realistic. Then, if it does better than anticipated, that's terrific. Whatever the promises, there should be facts and figures to back them up in a form that can be examined by you, your attorney and your accountant.

Financial Planning

Every general partner must understand financial planning. This background is needed to decide what he can or cannot handle. It's also needed in his relationship with you, so he can go over your financial statement with you and make sure you aren't investing too much of your money with the group. He can help you establish what your borrowing limits should be and be sure your financial goals are compatible with what he is offering.

Knowing the City

General knowledge about city planning is a must, but the general partner must also understand the specific city you're investing in so that he can check around—which includes a review of the city's master plan for growth—to determine the right location in the city in which to invest. He must be able to understand, interpret, and use population studies in selecting a site.

There are cases of general partners who put together purchases of neighborhood shopping centers, then were surprised a year or two later when a regional shopping center turned up on the next block—a possibility that could have been determined easily beforehand. The result, of course, is that shoppers switch from the neighborhood center to the regional center, and the limited partners then watch their profits die as the businesses disappear.

Fees, Commissions, Participation

You need to get a clear, thorough explanation of the fees, commissions, and extent of participation of general partners—both new ones and old-timers. They obviously work for their money, and are entitled to fair payment for that work. But you should understand the whole transaction so you can decide for yourself if you are willing to go along with a particular general partner's arrangements.

Property Management and Records

Whether the general partner hires a manager or a property-management firm, or does the managing himself, it is crucial that he knows the basics about keeping a property in good shape at minimum cost. Sometimes preventive maintenance is necessary to save money. Sometimes it's a premature expenditure. Your general partner must know how to tell the difference.

If, however, a general partner has a dependable expert property manager on the team, there isn't as much need for the general partner to know absolutely everything. Still, he must have enough knowledge to direct the expert and to appraise that person's recommendations.

Record-keeping, too, can be delegated. But since excellent records are a must, the general partner should know enough to ensure that it is done accurately and legally. Of course, the annual report and tax preparation should be handled by a C.P.A.

General-Partner Participation

The general partner usually receives a percentage of the investment automatically. However, the general manager should think enough of the investment to make a capital contribution as well.

What if the limited partners want to get rid of the general partner? In every contract I've seen, there are several remedies for dealing with a bad general partner. In some cases the limited partners, by a majority vote, can take over the property themselves or select a new general partner from the outside.

Public Offerings

Public offerings are usually large, with thousands of investors. They are policed by the Securities and Exchange Commission. One of the criticisms of private offerings—the kind of offering we're discussing in this book—is that they aren't inspected carefully enough by the SEC.

In fact, though, some private offerings are subject to the same rules as public ones, and you should assure yourself that your general partner knows this and complies with the law. One of the basic ideas is that no general partner should accept investment funds from someone who will be wiped out if those funds are lost. That is, the general partner should be convinced that the limited partner can survive financially without that money. It is highly unlikely that the money will be lost if you investigate an investment carefully, but no one can positively guarantee that your money is invested risk-free.

Now you know where to find a general partner, how to evaluate one, and what his duties are. The next step to group-investment success is determining the kind of investment that's best for you.

5 Which Kind of Group Should You Choose?

A drive through any middle-sized town in America will indicate the wide range of potential investments. There are single-family homes, duplexes and triplexes, apartment buildings, free-standing stores, shopping centers, homes that have been converted to offices after a rezoning, multistoried office buildings, recreational sites, and more.

There are old buildings in need of fixing up, as well as ground that is just being broken for new construction. There are properties of every size and for a variety of prices. Some are owned by individuals, some by groups. Some are condominiums. Just about any kind of land or building, from Wyoming grazing lands to Wall Street skyscrapers, can be considered for group purchase.

Let's explore some of the most likely possibilities.

Single-Family Houses and Condominiums

This kind of investment is usually safe, especially now that supply has fallen far below demand. An investment group can expect a substantial appreciation in areas of the nation that have a growing population. Each of the limited partners can count on his share of tax deductions for expenses, interest, and property taxes.

There are some problems, however, with a single-family home or condominium as income property. One problem is that income is usually low or even nonexistent. After you deduct the basic loan costs and the expenses of maintaining the place, the remaining funds can be small, especially when divided among the partners. At the same time, you need substantial money reserves and careful management to keep the property in good condition.

Finding suitable tenants can sometimes be difficult. If careless tenants wreck a place, the investors must not only repair the damages but also try to get it ready for rental quickly so it doesn't stand idle for long.

This kind of investment is probably best for a small group just starting out. The general partner should manage it, since an outside manager's fee can eat up the little profit available. Of course, if the investors aren't interested in income, a professional property manager can be hired and the profit can be realized at the time of sale.

Apartment Buildings

Small apartment buildings have some of the same advantages and disadvantages as a single-family home or condominium. Larger apartment complexes are usually a more attractive investment, offering tax benefits, spendable income each month, and the potential of excellent value appreciation.

Here again there are problems. Good management is essential in an apartment complex. You'll need a skilled on-site manager to watch over the physical property. But management involves more than this. Attention must be paid to good record keeping, to projecting income and expenses, and to raising rents equitably.

Rent-control laws can dampen an investor's enthusiasm about apartment complexes, especially when expenses go up faster than rental income. Occasionally, through the intricacies of income-tax deductions, an investor actually does better when expenses rise above income. But most of us want some spendable return and rent control can chop that down.

Middle-income residential apartment complexes had been the mainstay of my own investment program, but with rent control—accompanied by inflation—I found the prices of these properties were too high when compared with their potential income. So I have moved toward business and commercial investments.

Retail Stores and Shopping Centers

This kind of investment can be an excellent hedge against inflation while offering an attractive income—provided you have good tenants with the right kind of leases. Desirable leases provide for tax increases, cost-of-living increases, percentage rent clauses, and common-area maintenance charges. These leases let your income from the property keep pace with inflation. A percentage rent clause sets out a minimum monthly rental that you can count on, plus a percentage of income from the store's sales above an established dollar amount. For instance, an ice-cream parlor in a shopping center might pay $2,000 a month rent *plus* 5 percent of gross sales above $5,000.

One of the greatest potential problems with retail-store and shopping-center investments is that in bad economic times the stores may go out of business—lease or no lease. This factor makes the investment somewhat riskier than a residence. People must have shelter, but they don't want a store if their business has failed and they have to go to work for someone else.

When you have a percentage rent clause and business is good, you will probably be a very happy investor. When you have to settle for the minimum rent, the smile will fade. And if you try to sell the property at a time when income is down, you are probably not going to get a good price.

With a shopping center you may also find that you don't have as high an income-tax deduction for depreciation as you would expect. That's because a large percentage of the purchase price is usually allocated to land, for parking—nondepreciable, according to Internal Revenue Service rules—rather than buildings.

Office Buildings

Office-building investments, too, are tied directly to the type of tenants and leases. Generally, leases for offices are for shorter terms than they are for retail stores, and usually they don't include the percentage rent clause on sales.

Although long-term leases offer you security because you can expect that income, they force you to guess what the going rates will be in future years, and sometimes you can be way off. An area can suddenly get "hot," which creates a big demand for offices. Tenant turnover can be a plus if office space is scarce because with each change you can increase the rent to the current rate and be ahead of the game despite the expense of fixing up an office when a tenant leaves.

Industrial Property

The purchase of industrial property requires still more care and analysis. A multipurpose property is usually better because it has greater flexibility. A single-purpose building can be a big handicap when you lose the key tenant and try to find a similar replacement. Beware of owning a factory that's perfect for making ball bearings but useles for making anything else.

Often an industrial building *is* single-purpose. When the tenant leaves, the building commonly stands empty for a long time. It is then more susceptible to vandalism and theft, and now you have the maintenance expense without the rental income.

Industrial property can be a good investment, however, for the group that is satisfied with a moderate yield and slower appreciation than residential or business properties provide. This kind of investment is especially attractive in a rent-control area, since rent-control laws don't apply to industrial sites.

Agricultural Property

If you can find an excellent farm manager, as well as a general partner who understands group investments *and* farming (on the specific type of property selected for the investment), agricultural land can be a good place to invest your money.

The United States is one of the few nations in the world that produces more farm products than its people use. Not only is the U.S. population growing, but the world population is increasing—and with it grows the need for American farm products. Spendable income from farms is usually moderate, however, compared with that from other investments, although farmland in many states does appreciate substantially.

There are other prospective group investments that I haven't described: oil and gas developments, recreational sites such as tennis clubs or golf courses, mobile-home parks, building on a vacant lot to suit a tenant. Each of these is especially dependent on a general partner with highly specialized knowledge.

You should satisfy yourself that your general partner has a good track record in the specific type of investment. Experience is the best—and possibly the only—way to avoid high risk.

Ways to Put Together a Group

I've already described some of the ways a general partner can put together a group purchase. The general partner can buy the property, take it in his or her own name, and then sell it to the limited partners. As I explained, this is great for the general partner: He or she gets the profit up front. But there is little advantage to the limited partners.

Therefore I prefer the second method—the simultaneous purchase of the property by the general partner and the limited partners. Although the general partner makes the down payment before forming the group, the actual purchase is made together. All the participants make their profits at the same time, and the general partner gets whatever fees, commissions, and/or earnings are due under the partnership agreement.

A third type of group is known as a blind pool, which means the group makes a nonspecified investment, selected by the general partner. You put your money into the group, as a limited partner, without specifying what property is going to be purchased. Obviously the key factor here is your trust in the general partner. It is essential in a blind pool that you know your general partner's credentials thoroughly. (Of course, you should know them in *any* investment.)

There are some advantages to the blind pool. The general partner knows what funds are available for a purchase and can make quick decisions. He can buy property at a low price *now.* Without this ability to act quickly, the deal might not be as good.

Another advantage is that the money collected can be diversified—used for several projects rather than just one. This factor reduces the impact of any one project that turns out to be a poor investment and thereby increases the odds for success.

There are safeguards in most blind-pool agreements. If your general partner makes an offer for a property you don't want to invest in, you can usually pull out. But if *you* happen to be the general partner, that's one of the big disadvantages. It's sometimes a case of "now you have the money, now you don't."

For the limited partners the major disadvantage is that you must depend on the general partner to choose well. It's true you can usually take your money out, but you might have missed an excellent opportunity somewhere else while your funds were tied up with this general partner. Another disadvantage is that the limited partners can't review the facts and figures of the offer beforehand.

A fourth type of group investment is called a joint venture.

As in any other group investment, there are two or more partners in a joint venture. Each partner brings to the partnership some special skill or expertise. Many big construction projects, for example, are joint ventures of the developer (who, among other tasks, finds the land and gets zoning approved), the financial institution (which puts up the cash), and the construction company (which builds the project).

There are smaller joint ventures, too. Someone who owns a vacant lot may go into a joint venture with a carpenter, a plumber, an electrician, and a painter. Each makes his contribution (the land and the various building skills), and together they share in profits, losses, and tax benefits according to the terms of their joint-venture agreement. They're usually responsible for development and management as well, which are also spelled out in the agreement.

In a joint venture money may not be an especially important factor. Each partner can put up the cash for his portion of the joint venture, or he can supply land, time, skills, or materials. (Joint ventures can also be put together for the purchase of existing property.) Unlike in the group investments involving general and limited partners, everyone in a joint venture has equal risk and liability, and is commonly required to spend time on the project.

To summarize, there are four kinds of groups:

1. General partner sells his or her property to the group.
2. General partner finds the property and puts together the group investment.
3. Blind pool.
4. Joint venture.

If you are conservative and have the available cash, you may want to consider another approach to group investing and join a group that makes an all-cash purchase. When you pay cash for a property, however, you eliminate a large part of your potential tax deductions—interest on the mortgages. You should also first consider what that money might have made in a money-market investment.

But there are also advantages. Perhaps the best are that you substantially reduce risk and increase yield. Two-fifths of your tenants in an income-producing property could move out and you'd still have enough income to pay the operating expenses (taxes and maintenance). Because no money is going to mortgage payments, the yield is higher. You should expect an income of at least 12 percent a year on your investment.

In the past a 10 percent down payment was standard—but no longer. Nowadays, a down payment of 30 to 50 percent is usually required. Because of soaring interest rates, an all-cash investment can be a solution for keeping risk low in a market in which credit is tight and mortgage interest high. All-cash investments can be used in a blind pool, in a joint venture, or in a general partner's group investment.

New Ideas

Whatever kind of property and group you choose, you should be aware of the difference a creative general partner can make. For one thing, he can provide alternatives to traditional investing.

It is often a good idea, for example, to convert a building to a residential, commercial, or business condominium if the time is ripe and the price is right. One property divided into many individually owned apartments, offices, or stores can often provide the group investor with much more profit than a one-buyer sale. Being creative can mean taking a warehouse and converting it into condominium units. That takes work—and planning and imagination. But it's the kind of work that can make you a great deal of money.

A recent issue of *Real Estate Investing Letter* discussed recycling real estate. In Boston an old harbor warehouse was transformed into luxury condominiums with commercial shops on the ground floor. A former cotton warehouse in Oxford, Mississippi, became a small shopping mall. In Pittsburgh a sixty-year-old building that had housed an auto-repair shop and a movie theater was made into a group of fashionable boutiques.

Dividing a large lot into smaller lots is another good idea. Subdividing a large parcel into smaller parcels has the same advantage as condominiums: Instead of one buyer, there are a number of buyers whose total purchases amount to more than an individual might pay.

Another point to consider is that rental increases automatically establish a higher value for the property. When you look for property, you judge an acceptable price as a multiple of the gross income. If the income is higher, the property value is higher. For example, if the gross income is $100,000 a year and a buyer is looking for a purchase at seven times gross, he is willing to pay $700,000 for the property. If that gross income is $120,000 a year (a moderate increase), the price moves to $840,000.

A wise general partner can also frequently develop a construction project beyond the original expectations. Sometimes a piece of land is being used in a way that brings in an acceptable return—but nothing exceptional. With construction and development—say, of a gas station—the profit might be much higher. Often you can double the return by converting the property to a small shopping center.

Rezoning for a "higher and better use of land" is another good idea. Sometimes a property could be far more valuable and profitable to the investors if it were used for a purpose other than those the zoning laws permit. For instance, if you can obtain a variance for an apartment building in an area adjoining commercial property, the building can be converted into office suites at higher rents. But be prepared for trouble. Obtaining a variance in permitted use of land or a building is likely to be a long process, and may prove to be impossible if there is strong local resistance.

When a property has served its original purpose for the group, the smart general partner seeks to sell it or exchange it for a property more suitable to the new goals of the investors. The property can be sold to another group by the original general partner, who arranges a sale that is good for both groups. He should be equally savvy in a property-exchange negotiation.

I think the most exciting part of real estate investment is doing things that have never been done before or doing things *better* than they've been done before. In the neighborhood where I work, for example, somebody got the idea of building under a freeway ramp in a good central location that wasn't being used.

Flexibility, ingenuity, and creativity are crucial when you attempt to put people and property together in a unique way. The story of a woman I'll call Susan, who wanted to be a general partner, can serve as a good illustration.

Susan, an English teacher, had studied real estate in

night school for several semesters, fitting the classes into her busy schedule. She was eager to supplement her income and was willing to use her free time. But she didn't want to use her real estate knowledge to sell property. She wanted to be an investor. Since she had only $3,000 in savings, she decided to form a group and serve as the general partner.

It took Susan many months of reading ads and visiting properties after school and on weekends before she found a good buy—three stores on a single lot that fronted a busy street in an older part of town. All were on month-to-month leases at rents that were below the going market rates.

Susan put a group together, got the down payment, and completed the purchase. Then she put on an old shirt and a pair of blue jeans and painted the stores. She also saw to it that necessary repairs were made; they were minor, a fact she'd learned by checking everything out before making the purchase. When the stores were ready, she asked the tenants to lease them at a higher rent. Two agreed and the third store was quickly leased to a new tenant.

Then Susan had an inspiration. She subdivided the single lot the stores were on into three smaller lots and, fourteen months later, sold them at a good profit. The stores looked attractive, there were prosperous tenants in each of them (with leases that gave the new lot owners income right away), and the price of one-third of the large parcel was more than the whole would have been—but within the budgets of the three different buyers.

The possibilities in developing properties and adapting buildings to new uses are as rich as ever, as are the opportunities for investors.

6 How to Tell a Good Property from a Lemon

When I first started investing in real estate, I was overwhelmed. The thought of putting a large part of my available money into property was both appealing and scary. As a neophyte, there was so much I didn't know.

One of the first things I discovered was that not only automobiles can be lemons. A car can have a leaky radiator; a house can have leaky plumbing. A car can look handsome but have dozens of serious defects inside. So can an apartment house. It is vital to know how to tell a good piece of property from a lemon.

Probably the most important part of real estate investing is deciding which property to buy. Since everything hinges on finding the right property, I'm going to share with you the things I have learned about making such judgments, so that you can make your choices based on facts instead of fancy.

Investment property is a product. Thinking of it that way makes choosing far less mysterious. After all, you make decisions about products every day in your business and personal life.

There are six major points to consider before investing in residential apartment property:

1. Location.
2. Condition.
3. Price.
4. Financing.
5. Design.
6. Size.

Location

Location is without question the single most important factor in selecting a place to live. First you must select the city, then the part of the city, and finally the street.

Out-of-town or even out-of-state investments can be profitable because you can seek places where dynamic long-term growth patterns promise a demand for middle-income apartment housing that will be consistent and high. But it can be costly to travel long distances to watch over your property.

I started out with a small investment close to home,

and it was only after I began making larger investments that I went out of state. I live in California, where prices for property are skyrocketing. I decided to sharpen my investment skills and look elsewhere.

I headed for the Sun Belt and ended up in Texas, where I could still get a very good deal for myself and my investors. But if you're new at group investing or if you can't or won't travel, you can still do well in your own city.

Whether the city is near or far, however, you should consider the other important location factors.

First, buy on a main street, especially if it has other apartment buildings on it. Avoid dead-end streets. People may *talk* about a quiet little place at the end of a peaceful road, but they *rent* places where the action is—and where they have easy access to highways, shopping, and recreation. If other apartments are nearby, potential tenants for *your* place will be driving by day and night.

Second, buy a building that's visible. Most renters want maximum accessibility. They don't like apartment buildings set back from the street. They don't want to go down a long driveway.

Third, choose a property that's centrally located, close to the goods and services your tenants will need. If your tenants have children, are the schools, parks, and day-care centers nearby? If you have only adults in the apartments, can they get to shopping, services, and recreation easily? If your tenants are elderly, is the building near medical services and bus lines?

Fourth, visit the city's planning department, and ask to see its master plan for the area you're considering. An obvious question to ask is whether a highway is being planned that will go through the middle of a building you're interested in.

There are other things to find out at the planning department. Talk to the staff about the greatest growth area in the city, and inquire about any promising master-plan ideas that could benefit you (say, a shopping mall or highway). A word of caution: City master plans can be overblown, full of chamber-of-commerce hyperbole.

It is essential that you also find out what the zoning laws and building codes are now, as well as what the projections are. (I learned about building codes in the nick of time. I usually suggest buying buildings with no fewer than eight to ten units, but I had seen a little five-unit beauty that was just too good to pass up. I was about to close the deal when I discovered that the law limited use to a maximum of three units. So much for the five-unit beauty. It would have been a real beast if I had had to tear down two units or do battle with the city council to keep them.)

Fifth, check what's going on in the community. Some communities don't have jobs available for the middle-income apartment dweller you want to attract. Or the area isn't attractive enough to get people to commute to their jobs from there. In other cases communities become too expensive for the middle-income people who work there, and they leave not only their housing but sometimes their jobs as well. Jobs and apartments go begging then, so it's best to stay away from areas with these problems.

Sixth, try to avoid buying in rent-control areas. If you want to avoid a big headache, don't buy in an area where rent-control laws are in effect. Rent control could be the wave of the future, but right now there are plenty of places without it, where you can make a good investment *and* be fair to your tenants.

Seventh, catch the location at the right development cycle—the one you *want* to catch. Basically, here's how it works: There are certain development cycles (or value cycles) for real estate. There is the period of growth, when property values escalate. Then there is a plateau of slow growth or even no growth, followed by a period when values drop. Studies show that each cycle usually runs about twenty years.

There are reasons for buying at any part of the cycle, depending on your investment goals. The investor who wants an income from the property should buy just as value starts to go up and sell before the flattening out or decline in value.

In addition to the usual cycle, there are some brief bounces up and down that occur because of current economic or political situations. An energy crisis can put a strain on the suburbs, where commuting to work is a factor. A local factory closing can hurt an area until a new industry comes in. Inflation can cause some people to downgrade their housing or fall behind in rent payments.

You should be prepared to weather those relatively brief declines by having emergency money. Also, if you bought at six or seven times gross, you should be able to handle a vacancy factor as high as 20 percent and still break even. (I'll explain the phrase "times gross" shortly.)

Let me illustrate this point by describing an experience I had: One month after I had purchased a ten-unit apartment house in a middle-income area of Los Angeles' thriving San Fernando Valley, more than half my tenants gave notice. Alarmed, I rushed to talk to them. They assured me that it wasn't anything personal. Each of those apartments had at least one resident who was employed at a local aerospace company that had just permanently closed its doors. So there I was with a more than 50 percent vacancy factor, and the rest of the tenants were out of work.

I immediately dropped rents and converted the building from "adults only" to "families with children welcome." I wasn't undercapitalized. I had an emergency fund and now drew on it to cover the vacancy losses for the month or two it took me to fill the building again. I also put in a small play area for the kids.

The area got a boost from the opening of a big industrial and commercial center. (The city planning department had told me about it when I was first considering the purchase.) A year and a half after I'd made my investment, I sold the place and doubled my investment capital.

To summarize, when you're looking for a good investment, use common sense and consider the following:

- Buy on a main street.
- Buy a visible building on a through street.
- Be sure the property is well located for tenant conveniences.
- Talk to the city planning department.
- Find out what's happening in the community.
- Avoid rent-control areas.
- Buy in a neighborhood that's increasing in value.

Condition

There are two rules to remember about the condition of the investment property:

1. Buy the worst building in the best neighborhood.

2. Find a property with the right things wrong with it.

If you've ever bought used merchandise or seconds, you already know about finding goods with the right things wrong with them. How does this idea apply to property?

Cosmetic surgery on real estate, for example, is relatively inexpensive. If the place needs paint, if the fixtures are old or broken, if the landscape looks more like a moonscape, or if the general maintenance is poor, it may be a terrific investment opportunity. The property will be hard for the owner to sell, but you can make a profit by putting relatively little money into fixing it up.

This is especially true when it's the worst building in the best neighborhood. (Remember, "best" doesn't always mean the most expensive.) You can plant trees, put in a rock garden, mend a fence, put in new fixtures, give the building a painting, and send in a well-muscled crew to clean up. When that's all done, the place will sparkle and the tenants' morale will improve considerably.

Now that you've made the place more habitable, you can probably raise rents by a reasonable amount without having the tenants rebel. That's because there's another right thing wrong with such a property: low rents. If a building has had a zero percent vacancy rate for quite a while, it may be sending a message that rents are too low.

Most of the tenants will know they've had a bargain. Some might leave, but others will just accept the inevitable. I feel strongly, though, that you should *never* try to make your profit through excessive rent hikes. A 10 percent increase a year on an average building—and even more when you've worked hard to make it look and run well—is reasonable.

Watch out for property with the *wrong* things wrong with it. Stay away from buildings that have weak foundations, bad wiring, poor plumbing, structural problems, bad design that can't be changed, or serious violations of the building code. (If you don't have the expertise to judge if a place is in good shape and needs only cosmetic repairs, you should hire an expert to check it out.) Avoid a bad neighborhood that doesn't show signs of getting better.

If you're now convinced the property is a good deal, be sure the price you pay fully takes into account the cost of fixing what's wrong. And don't underestimate the time or money involved. You may have to put out all the tenants to do the repairs (if there are no local legal restrictions prohibiting temporary evictions), and repairs can take months. You could be spending money for a long time with no return.

Price

One of the obvious things to look at before selecting a property is its price. Even if you're a limited partner in the group, you should be aware of what makes a price right. Draw on some of that free advice real estate brokers offer. It's free because commissions are paid by the seller, not by the buyer. So ask away. I do and I find it's a big help.

The good brokers in an area can tell you about the fair market value of income property. They usually know what rents are being paid, as well as the general apartment-housing situation in the neighborhood.

After you get this information, compute how much your group should be paying for a particular place. (I'm convinced that since the invention of the pocket calculator, I look much smarter. With it I'm an instant whiz at figures. When the calculator's batteries run down and I try to do all that arithmetic mentally, I feel as if my IQ has dropped twenty points.)

There are a number of things to consider when you calculate a fair price (I'll discuss each of them in the chapter on negotiating), but for the preliminary stages of choosing a property, you really just need a good rule-of-thumb formula. The one I suggest you use is called "times gross," and it involves simple multiplication (and a few seconds with a pocket calculator). You take the actual gross income from the property and multiply it by 6, 7, and 8. Any price in that range is well worth considering. Let's take as an example the Heaven-Sent Apartments, which grosses $32,873 a year and is being offered for $350,000. Is that a fair price? Let's calculate:

6 times gross = 6 × $32,873 = $197,238
7 times gross = 7 × $32,873 = $230,111
8 times gross = 8 × $32,873 = $262,984

The price for the property is too high at 10.65 times gross ($350,000 divided by $32,873 = 10.65). If you really want this property, you should offer between $197,238 and $262,984 for it (6 to 8 times the gross).

There are many other basic pricing figures beside "times gross" that you should consider when you look at an income property for investment. Mortgage payments, for example, are important, and should be at most 50 percent of the gross income. The other operating expenses should be no more than 45 percent. Find out the current owner's rate on these expenses. Obviously, anything you can save from mortgage and operating costs becomes additional profit. You'll probably be able to get a yield of 5 to 10 percent on your investment (a conservative estimate), not counting tax benefits and appreciated value.

Another important factor is, is the seller flexible? What does the seller need? If you know that, you know where to give and where to hold fast.

Terms and conditions, another factor, can be more important than the actual price. If the seller needs tax benefits, make use of that information. The terms can be written to work in his best interests even if he accepts a lower price. If a seller needs to get out fast for some reason, a speeded-up purchase could mean a lower price for you.

Financing

The days of super-low down payments are behind us; today there is more demand for financing and less money available for it. But don't moan about the good old days: Become creative in financing. Your group should know the basics of financing so you can negotiate wisely.

One way to avoid high interest rates is to take over the existing mortgage on the property. There are several names for this procedure, but generally it is called an all-inclusive trust deed or a wrap-around mortgage. The seller lets you take over the existing mortgage at either the rate it was written (sometimes well below the current market rate) or at a higher rate that may still be below current market interest rates.

Then the seller takes up the difference between the selling price and the money from the old mortgage and down payment and wraps it all together. Here's a simple example of how it works:

Purchase price	$ 100,000
Down payment (20%)	– 20,000
Balance	80,000
Existing mortgage interest rate (8%)	– 60,000
Balance to be financed by seller at 10% interest	$ 20,000

The second mortgage's interest rate usually will be closer to the current interest rate. In some states the rate is controlled by usury laws that limit the amount.

Notice that even though the first mortgage has an interest rate of 8 percent, the seller's interest rate is 10 percent. When a mortgage is wrapped, the interest rate on all the money owed is at the higher figure, 10 percent. This means the seller will make an extra 2 percent for his efforts in making the payments and retaining the original financing.

Financing provides the basis for enormous flexibility in negotiating and it is easier to work out better deals as you get into the higher dollar brackets. But you can still be creative and negotiate even on single-family home investments.

You can probably work out the best, most flexible financing packaging if you have a large amount to invest. If you're like me, though, you'll start small. Then, as you keep trading up, you start having bigger and better negotiating power. You and your group have to start somewhere, and wherever it is, you should aim for the best financing available.

Design

The next factor to consider in selecting your property is the design of the apartment building and its grounds. Does the building have enough parking for tenants? If street parking is restricted, is there at least some space for the cars of guests or prospective tenants? If the community is one in which most people own cars, this is an important consideration. (I'm always hesitant about investing in a place where I end up driving around the block six times before finding a parking space.) Covered parking usually gets higher rent than open parking.

How flexible is the property? That is, can you add features to make it more rentable and more profitable now—and more attractive to a buyer later?

Does the design of the building and apartments meet the demands of potential tenants in the community? Rows of small, tidy apartments in classic motel style will rent well in a transient, singles-dominated town like Las Vegas. But they'd be hard to rent in Houston and other cities where even the singles market demands green spaces, stylish settings, large closets—the requirements of an area of solid but stable growth, where people are settling down and want their apartments to be home.

Size

Another thing to remember when you choose your group property investment is that big isn't always better. True, there are fewer buyers competing for a larger, more expensive building, so you can call more of your own shots with the lenders. (And the tax benefits and profits are often increased by raising the size of the investment.) But small can be good, too. And when you're a *group* investor, you're bigger right away. (As part of a group I was able to buy into more profitable property than I'd ever have managed by myself.)

Not everyone can afford a big or even medium-sized property, even in group investing. Set a reasonable target for now and work your way up to larger investments. Generally it's best to invest in at least an eight- to ten-unit apartment building. But start wherever you can afford to start. Your group investment can begin with a single house or with a four-unit apartment house. The main thing is to get started. Besides, bargain hunting is a special challenge when you have a limited budget.

Rent Control

Whole books could be written about the pros and cons of rent control, but the point here is how it relates to your group investment in middle-income apartment housing. For the prospective investor, rent control can be deadly.

My best advice to you is to stay away from investing in rent-control areas. But that isn't always practical or possible. These areas may become harder and harder to avoid if rent control spreads. The question, then, is how can you invest wisely in a rent-control area?

One way is to buy property beyond the rent-control authority. For instance, deluxe apartment housing usually has the advantage of being outside rent-control regulations, but of course it is also more expensive to buy.

Or you can buy "undesirable" property in an area that you expect will become more desirable, such as an inner-city building. You can buy property in need of renovation, move all the tenants out (if the law permits it), redo the place, and then rerent at higher prices. Obviously this involves a lot of money up front and there's some risk that you may overestimate the potential of the property. You also must be careful not to draw criticism—justly or unjustly—for putting poor people out into the street. There has been a lot of movement out of the suburbs and back to the central cities across the nation, however, and this may be the way to get around rent-control problems.

Those who have suffered most under rent control

bought property at as much as thirteen and fourteen times gross under the assumption that appreciated property values would result in higher rents. I know people who poured thousands of dollars a month into the property above the income they got from it, then were confronted with rent control and the fact that rents could *not* go up. All they can do to get out from under the expense is sell or convert to condominiums if possible.

Real estate is an interesting challenge because there are always creative solutions and alternative opportunities. So if you have rent-control blues, and you don't want to buy and fix up an "undesirable" or invest in a high-priced building, there's another solution besides putting your money in a sock under the mattress.

Industrial and Commercial Property

Move out of residential investments for a while, until the market turns around, and put your money into industrial and commercial real estate. There are problems here, too, but there are definite advantages during rent-control times. With industrial and commercial investments you'll usually get a lower yield on your investment capital, and it will take longer for the property value to grow. There's also a greater risk of long-term vacancies. But once you have a tenant, you usually have that occupant for a long time—and with fewer management problems than you have with residential tenants.

Broker's Listing Sheet

Before you buy a property, you need to read (perhaps I should say decipher) a broker's listing sheet, which is the piece (or pieces) of paper that informs you about the properties he is offering. Each property has its own sheet, which supposedly gives you all the things you need to know to make an intelligent decision about whether or not it's a good deal and if it's what you and your group are looking for. It's supposed to give you figures on income and expenses, plus many important details.

Reading a broker's listing sheet (or an owner's specification sheet if the owner is selling directly) can be an art, guaranteed to amuse and bemuse you—not to mention confuse and irritate. There is no standard form. It can be handwritten with a few numbers on it or it can be a handsome portfolio of information, bound and embossed in gold leaf. Here, too, big isn't necessarily better. No matter what size or shape it's in, it isn't going to be much use to you if it isn't based on hard facts rather than wishful thinking.

First check the broker's listing sheet you receive to see if rental income is referred to with the phrase "pro forma," "gross potential," or "rental projection." If it is, start getting nervous. They all mean the same thing: The figures given are what the seller and/or broker would *like* rents to be. They may not be close to the actual rents.

You want to know actual rents, and not only for the newest tenants but also for those who have been around a year or longer. If you make an offer to buy, you want to see a rent roll listing each tenant, the amount he actually pays, how much security deposit or other money is held on his behalf, and how long a lease (if any) he has and when it ends. The rent roll should be signed by the seller, certifying its authenticity. In the meantime, when you're at the earlier stages of considering the purchase, you want to know the true income rather than the wished-for income.

When you start reading a broker's listing sheet, seek out all the information. Start asking yourself—and the broker or seller—questions right away. If the sheet covers all the points that should be dealt with, that's great. But the odds are painfully high that it won't and you'll need to dig for more information. Keep these ten points in mind:

1. Make sure the sheet lists real income. Do not rely on a gross potential or a pro-forma figure.
2. If the gross potential rents are dreams, the gross potential income might be a dream, too. Check everything out.
3. Be sure you understand all the elements that are included in the income figure. It could be money from vending machines and laundry, plus rents—but you could also be looking at a one-time receipt of money from an insurance loss. Get an explanation of anything that is thrown into a category like "miscellaneous income," and don't accept vague responses. Get specifics.
4. An allowance of 5 percent for vacancy and credit-loss factor (bounced checks) is fair. If it isn't included on the listing sheet, you should figure it in yourself.
5. You want to know how many of each type of apartment is in the building (one-bedroom, two-

bedroom, studio) and the size of each, in square feet. You want to know the total square footage of all the units as well as the lot size.

6. Does the apartment have any green space, any parking? How many buildings are there? How old are they? What is the address? Is the property near cross streets, schools, major industries? All this should be on the listing sheet.

7. Don't settle for a "rough sheet" of expenses. Get itemized information. You want a list, naming each item—such as pool maintenance, repairs, cost of management, advertising—over the past year. All expenses should be listed separately. How old are the roof, the plumbing, and the paint job (inside and out)? You should pro-rate their replacement or repair costs into the expense to get an accurate picture, because you'll need to have a fund set aside for the major repairs that might be required during the time your group owns the property. Usually an older building is going to cost more for maintenance and repair than a newer building. (I estimate as high as 10 percent on an older building.)

8. Once you've made an offer, you must see the property's books so you can figure out what the expenses will be. For now, add 7 percent more for increased taxes and maintenance costs during the first year you'd own the property. (Yes, buyers can and do ask to see the books before making an offer, but the common practice is to make an offer—limited by several contingencies—and then check the books, records, and condition of the property.)

9. Taxes should be broken down into land and improvements. Before you complete a purchase, you also want to see the tax bill to be sure there aren't

any hidden items, such as a city assessment for a new water main.

10. You need to know what the current financing is, how many mortgages are against the property, who holds them, what the interest rates are, what the terms of sale might be, whether the loans can be refinanced, whether the seller will carry back any paper. ("Carry back paper" means the seller lends the buyer part of the purchase money and holds a wraparound mortgage.) You will want all of this information in writing, not just from talking with the broker or seller. Watch out for short-term balloon payments because you don't want to invest all your money and find you're obligated to make a big balloon payment in a few years. (A short-term balloon payment is a big chunk of money that has to be paid back in a short time.) Give yourself as much time as possible to pay off mortgages.

Below is a checklist of what to look for on a broker's listing sheet:

- Age of the building.
- Size of the lot.
- Address.
- Number of buildings.
- Number of units.
- Square feet per unit.
- Types of apartments.
- Extra items (swimming pool, rec room).
- Actual rents received.
- Total income (including laundry, vending machines).
- Personal property owned, if any.

- Breakdown of tax bill by land and improvements.
- Number of mortgages and terms.
- To whom the mortgages are payable.
- Interest rate.
- Terms of sale.
- Can property be refinanced?
- Will seller carry back paper?
- Real expenses (checked against the apartment's books before you actually buy) for all items over the past year, including taxes, utilities (who pays the apartment utilities?), management, advertising, all repairs and maintenance, insurance, vacancy and collection losses.
- What are the existing lease terms, if any?
- What security deposits and other moneys are being held?
- What reserves do you need to pay for potential major repairs?
- Estimate of your first-year costs for taxes and utilities, and assume costs will go up.)
- Total costs of necessary repairs and maintenance.
- What are the chances of increasing rents? (Check on what tenants are paying for similar apartments nearby.)

Now you know how to tell a good piece of property from a lemon, and it's time to take the next step: raising the money to invest.

7 Increasing Your Investment Capital

Sometimes finding the cash you need to join a real estate investment group is simply a matter of knowing where to look. And sometimes it requires some thinking to figure out which of your assets can be converted to cash.

One of the common sources of investment cash is equity, the difference between the current market value of your property and the balance due on the mortgage. If you own your home or other property, you may have equity that can be used as collateral for a loan; an appraisal will tell you the size of that equity. Then check with several lenders to find where you can get the best loan at the best interest and the best terms. After that it's just a matter of being sure you can repay the second mortgage.

Perhaps you have extra income but just don't have the lump sum needed for the investment. Then it won't matter as much if your group investment doesn't provide enough income to cover your second-mortgage payment. Otherwise you will want to be sure your investment provides it. This factor should be a primary consideration in selecting a group. Make sure the group will give you income to meet the costs of borrowing investment money.

Another way to raise cash is to sell all or some of your stocks and bonds, including U.S. Savings Bonds. Historically, real estate investments have brought better returns than stocks and bonds.

Credit cards issued by banks sometimes include a cash-advance privilege. This arrangement is usually good for only a few thousand dollars at most, but it may be the source of a quick loan if that's all you need to bring your total high enough for your share in the group.

If your life-insurance policy allows you to borrow against it, you can usually do so at a below-market interest rate. Frequently people borrow against their insurance because (a) it's a relatively inexpensive loan and (b) it's money that isn't "earning its keep" unless you borrow it and invest it. Another source of funds is canceling unnecessary policies. Not only can you save the additional premiums, but in some cases you can qualify for a refund of previously paid premiums. Other policies have a cash value you can redeem.

The bank may give you a personal loan based on your good credit. This is called a signature loan—the bank lends you the money without collateral. All you're required to do is sign the loan documents and, of course, pay back the money. Credit unions are another source of personal loans, and frequently they lend at a favorable interest rate.

Does the federal government or your state or local government owe you money? An income-tax refund can be used as seed money to get you started with a group. Or you may qualify for a property-tax refund under a homestead, senior-citizen, or veteran's exemption.

Relatives are often willing to lend family members money for good, solid investments. Sometimes a relative will make an outright gift of money. In fact, there are definite tax advantages for most people if they give money to their children and grandchildren rather than have them receive everything as an inheritance. Each parent can give a child or grandchild up to $10,000 (for a total of $20,000) a year free of gift tax. Ask your accountant to take a look at your specific circumstances and advise you and your relatives.

Maybe there's an uncollected debt that's owed to you. Calling in overdue loans is another way to get the money you need.

If there is a settlement due you from an inheritance or a lawsuit, it may be economically wise for you to get a loan now by using that future payment as collateral. If the group investment is a good one, you could earn more by getting in right away rather than waiting for a group purchase to come along after your settlement is paid on its regular schedule. Be careful, though. Many regular lenders won't make this kind of loan. You want to be sure that the lender will give you a fair deal, and you also want to be certain your inheritance or settlement is indeed going to be paid to you.

Perhaps you can cash in your unused sick leave or

vacation time or retirement plan at your job. If you have a Keogh or an IRA plan, however, cashing it in is going to cost you penalty fees. But for the right investment it might be worth it.

If you don't need a sizable amount of additional cash, a garage sale could bring in the money you need—and clear out your closets at the same time. Or maybe you don't need cash at all. A second trust deed might be accepted in lieu of cash for your share of the group purchase.

Below is a cash-source checklist:

- Refinance your home or other property.
- Sell stocks and bonds.
- Cash in U.S. Savings Bonds.
- Get a credit-card advance.
- Borrow against insurance policies.
- Get a loan from your bank.
- Get a loan from your credit union.
- Borrow against a settlement from a lawsuit.
- Borrow from relatives.
- Get tax-wise gifts from relatives.
- Cancel unnecessary insurance policies.
- Use homestead, senior-citizen, or veteran's exemptions for a property-tax refund.
- Collect bad debts you let slip by.
- Hold a garage sale.
- Cash in retirement funds, sick leave, vacation time.
- Use a second trust deed for a new purchase.
- Use your income-tax refund.

You hear a lot about creative financing, and I want to encourage you to consider how you can gather money to invest. The story of how one couple did so can serve to illustrate the point.

Jeff and Linda owned a large home. After their children were grown and on their own, the couple felt the house was too big for just the two of them.

They were interested in group investments and in fact felt they had the time and know-how to be general partners for a group consisting of themselves and some friends. The major problem was getting together enough cash to start the ball rolling. Rearing three children and helping them through college had depleted their savings.

Jeff and Linda moved out of their house and into a comfortable apartment in town. They leased the house for a year, which brought in more than enough cash to cover the apartment rental and the low mortgage payment on the house.

Then they started learning even more about group investments, real estate law, and real estate in general. And they kept their eyes open for a good potential investment.

Fourteen months later, they were ready to make their move. They found a buyer for their home, which now qualified as income property. But instead of selling, they exchanged the equity in the house for their share of the income property they had selected for their group's investment. Not only did they get the money they needed, but they also deferred the taxes on the profits gained from the sale of the house. As principals and general partners they legally qualified to make this exchange of "like for like"—income property for income property.

Because Jeff and Linda were creative, they found the money they needed, thereby achieving their additional goal of becoming general partners in a real estate group. The group showed excellent promise of growing and expanding beyond its first income-producing property purchase.

To gain an idea of how a $25,000 investment might be used in some of the alternatives to real estate, check the figures in the chart on pages 100 and 101.

Obviously some of the figures shown are subject to a changing market, such as the return on money-market investments, the average return from stocks and bonds, and so forth. But the figures are relative to one another, and to that extent they are representative.

I'll emphasize the point again: Real estate group investments can outproduce other investments that have similar foundations of strength and security.

Financing the Property

The actual negotiations and arrangements for the loan are the responsibility of the general partner, but it's the kind of information all limited partners ought to understand for their own protection. Clearly, the wrong moves in financing a property can make or break an investment. For example, too-high interest rates can gobble up any potential profits.

When I began to write this book, I decided it would be interesting to reflect on what the economic forecasters and other seers were saying at the beginning of the last decade, the decade of the '70s. I discovered that I couldn't find a single forecaster who had accurately predicted what would happen to the real estate market. Nowhere did I find a forecast of the dramatic changes that affected real estate during that ten-year period: skyrocketing interest rates, a world energy crisis, runaway inflation.

Some saw pieces of the whole, but I found no one who had imagined the complete picture. I emphasize this point because I want you to keep it in mind when you read the predictions for real estate in the 1980s—including mine.

We can take a look at the past and use it as a guide to what might happen in the future, but the plain fact is no one really knows. That's why I prefer to look at the larger picture—what's happened over the past seventy to eighty years. Real estate has consistently been a good investment. The enormous profits realized by so many investors in the 1970s were uncommon in prior decades, but steady, reliable profit has been consistently achieved through the years.

The best advice I can give is to work with what the market offers right now, today. Creative financing can smooth out some of the highs and lows. I usually don't suggest buying investment property at the high-interest levels because it's possible, if you are creative, to find ways to buy at far more favorable rates. But terms can make the difference, too; sometimes they offset the negative aspects of higher mortgage interest. The mortgage market is the mainstay of the real estate market. As it goes, so goes the world of real estate.

The first factor in creative financing is the financial standing of the individuals who will be buying the property—you and your partners. The general partner's financial statement and credit rating are the most important, but lenders will usually want to know about the limited partners, too.

Certainly any general partner will need the reassur-

REAL ESTATE COMPARED TO OTHER INVESTMENTS
($25,000 based on a 40% tax bracket)

Type of Investment	Cash to Be Invested	Additional Costs or Expenses to Investor	Payments	Tax Benefits or Costs	Return on Investment (percentage)	Yearly Cash Yield	Total Yield per Year After Taxes*	Total Yield (percentage)
Savings accounts	$25,000			cost	5.25	$1,312.50	$ 787.50	3.1
Money market	25,000			cost	14	3,500	2,100	8.4
Second trust deeds	25,000	1%		cost	13 (net)	3,250	1,950	7.8
Stocks	25,000	brokerage commissions		cost	10	2,500	1,500	6

Bonds (AAA municipal)	25,000	commissions		no state or local income tax	7	1,750	1,050	12
Annuities (insurance, etc.)	25,000		premiums	benefit: tax-deferred	12	no yearly yield—paid at end		12
Real estate: $125,000 building (cost); $100,000 loan at 12% for 20 years	25,000		$13,212 on loan	Benefits: depreciation at 5% a year = $6,250; interest payments deductible: $12,000	25% (reduction of principal on mortgage, tax benefits, and estimated cash flow of 6%)	1,500 (6%)	6,350	25.4

*Including tax benefits or liabilities, appreciation, equity buildup, and cash flow, but not including state taxes.

ance that the limited partners have good financial standing. Even the general partner with a fine enough reputation to get loans without having to worry about the limited partners will need to know that the limited partners will be there when needed.

A limited partner's ability to come up with additional funds can be important—whether or not he is ever asked to do so. The unpredictability of the economy can mean extra cash is needed along the way to keep an investment above water.

When rent control becomes law retroactively in your area, for example, your income can drop below the projected figures. I've known groups that had made major expenditures—in a large swimming pool and landscaping, for example—to improve the property. Then they got hit with rent reductions and controlled increases, which meant more cash was needed to keep the investment going.

The next stage of financing is finding a lender. The general partner's ability to sustain and repay the mortgage is the main thing a lender will look at. But no matter what lender you go to, he is going to want to look at the whole transaction, including a tour of the investment property.

He'll usually have his assistants do a thorough job of determining if the property is being used well. They will decide if the purchase price is consistent with use and will compare the property to similar properties in the neighborhood.

They'll especially want to check out the income and expense figures. What is the income? If there is a lease, what are its terms? How responsible and reliable are the tenants? Can rents or other income be increased? What is the life of the building? Is the neighborhood in a downward or an upward spiral?

Financing Rules of Thumb

The main rule about financing: The monthly mortgage payments should never exceed 50 percent of the monthly income. You can probably assume the investment is questionable if that figure goes over 50 percent. The lower the cost of financing, the more profit is possible.

Later, when we explore the details of negotiating, you'll be using this 50 percent maximum as a guideline on limits. For now it's something to keep in mind when you start considering all the different ways to finance a property.

Conventional loans for income property are less and less frequent because of that unstable world of mortgage financing we have been living in for the past seven or eight years. The old saying about things getting worse before they get better seems to be true of mortgage financing. Maybe the worst is over by now, but maybe it's not.

With creative financing, however, you don't have to be as concerned with that question because you are in effect writing your own deals. You are working on a one-to-one basis, making the best possible arrangements for the specific property you want to buy. Every seller has his own needs and concerns, just as each group buyer does. Creative financing is simply enabling both sides to enter into a mutually acceptable agreement.

When mortgage interest rates began soaring out of sight, the wrap-around mortgage (also called the all-inclusive trust deed) became increasingly popular as a nontraditional form of financing. The basic idea is to have the seller keep his existing mortgage loan on the property. The seller, to provide an incentive to the buyer to make the property marketable, will stay on that original mortgage and will lend you the difference between the down payment and the first mortgage.

The key to this system is that the old mortgage, in a high-interest market, will be at a lower rate than the buyer could get by conventional means. The seller passes on this advantage to the buyers and makes it worth their while by getting a good interest rate on the part he carries back—the second mortgage.

Here's an example of how it works: An apartment house sells for $500,000. The down payment is $100,000. That leaves a balance of $400,000 to be financed. There's already a 9 percent mortgage loan totaling $300,000.

The seller agrees to pass that 9 percent mortgage on to the buyer at 10 percent and to carry the difference between it and the down payment ($100,000) in a "wrap"—a wrap-around or all-inclusive trust deed. The interest on the second trust deed is 12 percent

The seller has added 1 percent to the first mortgage because that mortgage remains his responsibility throughout the term of the first. The 1 percent makes it worth taking the risk that the buyer might default.

In the meantime, the buyer is paying a rate of 10½ percent on the $400,000 financed instead of the 12 percent rate then in effect at banks and savings-and-loan associations.

Everyone benefits, but you need to be cautious about balloon payments in arranging a wrap-around loan. The wrap-around will most likely require a balloon payment on the second mortgage in a relatively short time. It's important that you, as a group investor, be sure ample time has been allowed for your group to raise or make the money on the property to cover that balloon payment.

The Lender Joins

Lenders sometimes will agree to lend money at a lower rate in return for being allowed to participate. That's another form of nontraditional financing. Under this system the lender participates in the income from the property. He becomes a third party in the operation of the investment until the loan is paid off. The terms of such participation are spelled out in the financing agreement. Limited partners and general partners should examine those terms carefully.

The lender-participation method is especially good for a new development, which has a lot of expense and no income at first. Reduced interest rates help offset starting-up costs, which can be recovered later as rents start coming in.

Another lending technique is the sale and leaseback, which works for raw land as well as for developed property. In a sale/leaseback, the investor group buys the land from the seller, then leases it back to the seller on a long-term lease. The purpose is to give the investor tax benefits and other investment pluses while the seller has the use of the property without keeping his money in it. This method is usually recommended only if the seller-tenant has an excellent credit rating, and also involves significant tax considerations.

Sale/leasebacks can take another form. They can be set up so that the seller-lessee has an option to buy back the property. The investor agrees to the sellback price at the beginning, which may be an excellent benefit to the seller-lessee, since the property may appreciate faster than anticipated by the option sale price.

In a sale/leaseback the improvements on raw land are usually financed and developed by the seller-lessee. Then the investor steps into the picture.

Creative financing is also reflected in repayment terms. A mortgage can be written with smaller monthly payments for the first few years, growing gradually to the higher amount. For the investment group this means the higher mortgage payments come at a time when it can anticipate getting more income from increased rents.

You also can escape high mortgage loan rates by exchanging your property for another investment property, often with no cash changing hands. By exchanging two properties, the financing procedure can be limited to exchanging loan packages as well.

A cooperative broker will sometimes help the financing by putting his commission into the second trust deed. He's especially likely to do so if it's the difference between making a sale or not.

Another loan possibility is the Flexible Loan Insurance Program (FLIP). In this plan the buyer places a 10 percent down payment in a pledged savings account. This is an equity substitute for the down payment and for the monthly mortgage payments, with the lender advancing the full purchase price and using the savings account for withdrawals of the subsidized mortgage payments (subsidized in that the mortgage company is making the payments). Before five years have elapsed, the subsidy account is empty and the borrower makes the full payments directly. FLIP is generally used by young buyers who are unable to raise the down payment on a home. In a tight money market FLIP is less common.

Another form of creative financing is to purchase the improvements (usually buildings) and lease the land on which the improvements are constructed. The land leases are long term—usually one or more generations. Sometimes the buyer has an option to buy the land. The effect is to bring the cost of the purchased property down to an affordable level. But there are built-in hazards in not having true control, let alone ownership, of the land on which your building is constructed.

Short-term mortgages are more frequent in a high mortgage interest market. These sometimes take the form of roll-over mortgages—that is a total refinancing of the balance every five years or so. It's a way to avoid being locked into the high interest for the long haul, but there is the risk that the interest rate will be even higher at the end of the loan period—or, even worse, that you won't be able to refinance the property at that time and may lose it.

There is a lot of controversy about variable-rate mortgages—mortgages whose rates vary with the current market rate. The potential of the rate reaching levels higher than the buyer can afford is less of a problem to the income-property investor than to the home buyer. If you are making a group real estate investment, the odds are you'll be selling or exchanging that property within five years. This factor makes it easier to live with the uncertainties of a variable-rate mortgage.

When the headlines spell doom and gloom, try to remember that the real estate market has a lot of flexibility, a lot of room for creativity.

Where to Get Financing

The seller as lender has already been discussed. There are other sources, of course. And, again, some are traditional and some are not.

The most traditional sources in the United States are the savings-and-loan associations and other institutional lenders. Savings and loans are primarily in the business of making loans for housing, single units and multiple. They're your most likely source of housing loans.

The other types of institutional lenders are commercial banks, mutual-savings banks, and insurance companies. (Mutual savings banks are state-chartered institutions operating much like savings-and-loan associations in the states where they exist.)

Both savings-and-loan associations and commercial banks are state or federally chartered and are governed by regulations. All federally chartered institutions have the same rules, whereas the state-chartered associations and banks must comply with the rules of the state in which they operate. State-chartered lending institutions are limited to operating within their state except for those types of government-guaranteed loans that can cross state lines.

Specific state and/or federal laws limit the activities of institutional lenders and set rather rigid limits to what they can do. Most of those rules were made to protect borrowers and to safeguard against imbalances that could cripple the nation's economy.

There are other lenders with broader regulations and still others with almost no restrictions. All must adhere to maximum-interest-rate laws, however.

State governments also regulate insurance companies. In many states, such as California, any insurance company doing business there is subject to the state laws regardless of where the company's home office is. This regulation has affected the real estate market because where the ceiling on interest rates that an insurance company can charge is below its profit level, insurance loan funds are removed from that state's investors.

In 1980 California voters changed their usury law in a statewide referendum. Insurance-company loans were often unavailable in the state because the 10 percent interest limit was well below market rates, and voters wanted to open this channel of loan funds. In the past they had rejected any such change in the law, but they became almost desperate for ways to bring more lending funds into the state. They hoped for a reduction in overall mortgage interest rates because then there would be a greater supply to meet the demand. The voters chose what they considered the lesser of two evils—higher interest limits in exchange for potential lower interest rates. (However, interest rates did *not* drop.)

Mortgage bankers and mortgage companies have more flexibility than institutional lenders when they lend their own funds. They are then limited only as to the amount they can charge borrowers for costs and expenses, and must meet restrictions on the minimum amortization terms for loans involving balloon payments. (Amortization is the periodic repayment of a debt.) These mortgage bankers and mortgage companies have the same restrictions as institutional lenders when they act as agents or correspondents for such lenders. (A correspondent works for a mortgage company, putting lenders and borrowers together.)

More and more frequently, credit unions are getting

into long-term real estate financing. These are mutual, voluntary, cooperative organizations of co-workers. They are regulated but not as much as most other lenders.

There are private lenders, too—not sellers who agree to what amounts to a private loan, but people who are in the business of loaning money both directly and indirectly. They generally finance second mortgages of comparatively small amounts.

Some companies specialize in second-mortgage lending, too. They may be syndications of people who pool their funds to buy second mortgages. Other syndications and real estate investment trusts also may be lending sources for investment purchase money.

Until recently pension funds were usually invested in government securities and corporate stocks and bonds. Now, to diversify, more and more pension-fund managers are turning to real estate. They frequently take the lender-participation role.

Trust companies and the trust departments of banks and insurance companies are entrusted with funds from many sources—pension plans as well as estates, corporations, individuals, and others. They, too, are increasingly expanding their portfolios to include real estate investments, and are often a good source of interim and short-term loans.

Investment-counseling firms are also a source. Many include real estate investments in their clients' portfolios. They frequently join in purchases as limited partners.

We've discussed a lot of information about creative financing, money-gathering, and money-lending. Perhaps the quiz below will help to clarify some of the issues. Choose the answer or answers that come closest to completing the statement correctly.

1. In a high-interest market you should
   a. Back away and wait for rates to come down.
   b. Find financing that will bypass the high interest.
   c. Ask your bank for a special low-interest-rate loan because you have good credit.
2. The first step to take if you want to get a loan on the equity in your residence or income-producing property is to
   a. Estimate the equity and ask the savings-and-loan association for that amount.
   b. Ask your general partner to give you cash credit for the amount of the equity.
   c. Get an appraisal and see how much lenders will lend and under what terms.
3. If you get a second mortgage on your property, you should be sure that
   a. You get the loan from friends or family.
   b. There is no big balloon payment coming due before you're ready for it.
   c. You can make payments from the income of the group investment or from other extra income.
4. Actual financing negotiations and arrangements are handled by
   a. The limited partners.
   b. The general partner.
   c. The whole group, including general partner and limited partners.
5. The unpredicted major influences on the real estate market in the 1970s were
   a. High mortgage interest rates.
   b. Runaway inflation.

   c. Energy crunch.

6. If you do your financing creatively,
   a. You may never have to deal with an institutional lender.
   b. You should wait until interest rates hit high levels.
   c. You can ignore the rule of keeping mortgage payments no higher than 50 percent of income from the property.

Answers: 1—b (and *c* if you can get away with it); 2—*c;* 3—*b* and *c;* 4—*b;* 5—*a, b,* and *c;* 6—*a.*

8 The Use of Experts

Knowledge is your best protection against making mistakes in group real estate investments. You don't need to know all the answers, but because your second-best protection is the expert use of experts, you have to know what to ask.

Most people find an attorney invaluable, and frequently an accountant as well. If you choose to be a general partner, you'll need in-depth advice, so you'll want to expand your team of experts.

Just as you can't know it all, no one expert is likely to fill all your advisory needs. Occasionally an attorney will have an accounting background and also be knowledgeable about real estate investments and group purchases, but this type of lawyer is uncommon indeed.

Experts can more than pay for themselves because their experience can save you many thousands of dollars. Some charge a fee; others do not. It depends on their role. Lawyers and accountants bill you for the time they devote to your concerns. A real estate broker, on the other hand, provides services at no charge to you if you're the buyer. Only sellers have to pay commissions to brokers. Bankers charge for their services but frequently provide consultation for nothing.

All these experts have one thing in common: The right ones give you access to a good deal of important information *and* the additional value of a different point of view. Even if you are something of an expert yourself in some areas of group investing, you will benefit from a second opinion. (My attorneys, accountants, real estate brokers, and bankers have pointed me in the right direction many times, and are responsible for having saved me and my limited partners thousands of dollars.)

Choosing a Lawyer

What do you require in a lawyer? If you are a general partner, you need a great deal, but even a limited partner will be best protected if he has an attorney who is a specialist in real estate, who is experienced in putting together groups, and who thoroughly understands the laws of contract for the state he lives in.

As either a general or limited partner you want a responsive person who returns your phone calls, answers your questions without a lot of legal double-talk, and persists in solving problems. A rigid lawyer will not serve your purposes well because the nature of real estate investments makes flexibility—the ability to make deals rather than break them—of prime importance. Your lawyer should be aggressive and possess an open mind. He should search for acceptable alternatives rather than counsel you to hold your ground even if it means losing a very good opportunity.

Of course there are times when holding your ground is best, but usually there are ways to reach an agreement that satisfies all parties. You need an attorney who will look for that middle path, protecting your interests but understanding how to reach the goal.

I once had a rigid attorney. He carefully explained all the reasons why a particular project couldn't be put together, and his reasons all sounded logical. But when I lamented the incomplete deal to a friend, he suggested I see an attorney he'd heard about. I took that advice and the second lawyer found a perfectly acceptable way to bring the seller and me together. It was a good lesson. The first lawyer was reputable and capable but wrong for the role of legal expert in group real estate investing.

I strongly urge group investors to keep looking until they find an attorney who meets the necessary criteria: expertise in *real estate* law, firsthand group investment experience, flexibility, and a personality and style that suit the investor's needs.

Such a person may be recommended to you by a friend who's involved in group investments. Possibly the best source for a recommendation is a real estate broker. Go to the biggest real estate office in your community and ask the brokers there for the names of their attorneys. Chances are they have chosen experienced counselors who have a thorough knowledge of real estate.

After you have two or three names, arrange for interviews. Some lawyers charge for a preliminary interview and some don't. You should include that as a factor in deciding whom to hire. It could be a sign that getting your money has a higher priority than giving you service.

Be sure to talk to the attorney who would actually handle your business. You won't get a clear picture talking to a senior partner if his nephew, fresh out of law school, is the one who will be handling everything. If a junior partner is to be involved, request that he be in on the interview, too. (I'm using "he," but your lawyer, of course, could just as well be a woman.)

Begin your evaluation when you get to the law firm's offices. Do they exude an air of success, or are they merely pretentious? Are you kept waiting past your appointment time and, if so, for how long? How does the attorney treat his secretary? What feelings do you get from the office staff? Tuning in to them can reveal something about the law firm.

In the interview try to determine whether the lawyer understands what you're talking about. Does he focus on the questions you're asking? Are you expected to wait while he takes phone calls? If so, is any confidential information discussed within your hearing? Is the attorney discreet about keeping clients' papers out of view so that there's no chance of breaching confidentiality? Does the lawyer use a lot of technical or legal words that put you at a disadvantage, or does he give you straight talk?

The kinds of questions you ask will depend in part on your own experience and knowledge, but below are some of the essential points you need to cover and some questions you want to weave into the conversation (so that the lawyer doesn't feel as if he's on the hot seat):

- What is your experience in real estate law?
- Are you a real estate investor yourself?
- Have you invested with groups?
- Were you a general partner or a limited partner?
- Are you presently involved in a group real estate investment?
- What kind of property is involved?
- What types of real estate clients have you had?
- Can you tell me about some of your specific real estate law experiences?
- How do you feel about negotiating when the parties can't seem to agree?
- How have you managed to get through such obstructions with other clients?
- Would anyone else in your office handle my business? (If so, ask to meet him.)
- What do you charge?
- When and how do you bill?
- How many hours would you estimate it would take you to review a set of limited-partnership papers and give me your opinion?

Choosing an Accountant

If you like a lawyer and are considering using him, there's one other question you'll want to ask him: Can you recommend a good certified public accountant (CPA) with knowledge and experience in real estate taxes and accounting? If he can't, your lawyer and the accountant you select should get to know each other, either in person or by telephone, because they should be able to coordinate their efforts in your best interests.

Even if the accountant comes recommended, you should interview him because your own judgment about his ability and his compatibility with you and your style is important. The characteristics you want in an accountant are in some respects similar to those you require in an attorney. For instance, it would be helpful if he has had firsthand experience as a group real estate investor because he will be more in tune with your needs.

The most important point is experience in real estate accounting and taxes. It is crucial that the accountant know tax laws thoroughly, particularly those that affect acquisition and sale of property. He must also be informed about exchanges. In short, you need an accountant who specializes in real estate taxes and accounting.

Generally, I recommend selecting a certified public accountant because these accountants have to pass a stringent test to earn the right to use that title. I've found that big CPA firms that are household names—national firms with hundreds of CPAs working for them—aren't the most suitable for real estate investment groups because they tend to be ultraconservative in approach. They are concerned with protecting themselves against liability and avoiding anything that might be questioned.

The kind of CPA I prefer and recommend is one who will take *reasonable* chances. I'm certainly not suggesting that you look for a character who will hide income or play games with your books. But many, many areas of real estate tax law and investment strategy are subject to interpretation, and you want a CPA who will interpret something to your benefit if he believes it to be reasonable and fair—and, of course, legal.

When you interview a prospective accountant, observe whether he is well organized. If you have to wait while he removes a pile of accounting papers from one of the chairs before you can sit down in his office, be careful. That could be *your* paperwork at the bottom of the pile, getting shuffled around rather than properly handled.

Perhaps the most important quality for an accountant is his ability to weigh all the alternatives carefully and to list options for you. This ability is vital both in making the original investment and in filing tax returns later.

Once you've formed a preliminary opinion after seeing the accountant's office and staff, work these questions into the conversation with subtlety (accountants don't enjoy being grilled, either):

- What is your experience in real estate taxes and accounting?
- Are you a real estate investor yourself?
- Have you invested with groups?
- Were you a general or a limited partner?

- What professional organizations do you belong to?
- What steps do you take to stay current with changing real estate laws and tax regulations?
- What types of real estate clients have you had?
- Can you tell me about some of your specific real estate tax and accounting experiences?
- Have you challenged any tax rulings?
- How do you feel about taking risks in interpreting tax regulations?
- Can you supply me with several references—names of your real estate investment clients?
- Would anyone else in your office handle my business? (If so, ask to meet that person.)
- What do you charge?
- When and how do you bill?
- How do you see my role in our client-accountant relationship?
- To what extent would you spell things out for me concerning any alternative positions I might take?

The Uses of the Attorney and the Accountant

Since the general partner is the responsible party in any limited partnership agreement, it is the general partner who needs the most protection—protection that comes from the expert use of experts. If you are the general partner, I strongly suggest you hire both an accountant and an attorney. There aren't many people who can be experts in real estate law *and* tax law. The attorney will help you work out the best possible deal, and the CPA will prepare the offering to make sure investors get maximum benefits. The lawyer offers legal protection; the accountant offers tax protection and accounting services.

A good accountant also can provide valuable advice to limited partners by spelling out benefits of real estate investment clearly.

The limited partners must take responsibility for their own protection before signing any document. One frequently asked question in a partnership is, Can the general partner be replaced if the limited partners are unhappy with him? That question must be considered before the agreement is prepared and signed. In the contract I use, the limited partners always have the right. But in other contracts limited partners are forced to put up with an unsatisfactory general partner or get into lengthy legal tangles to try to cancel the agreement.

If a limited partner wants to sell out for one reason or another, the general partner needs legal expertise. The lawyer can prepare a release-of-liability form (see a California sample on facing page) that protects the general partner so that once the limited partner is paid, the general partner is released from any further liability or responsibility for that limited partner. Having a lawyer when dealing with such a matter can be a great help to a general partner.

Your lawyer and accountant are usually not able to say without hesitation that a general partner is or is not getting a fair share of the profit. There are many factors involved in making such a decision. But they will be able to give you opinions based on experience so that you can make your own judgment.

For all parties to a group investment the attorney

and accountant will be helpful in analyzing these questions:

- What are the economic pros and cons of the project now and in the future—the prospective income, expenses, and profit?
- Could better use of your investment dollars be made elsewhere?
- What are the income-tax ramifications of the project?
- Are the goals and objectives of the individual investors being met?
- Are the general partner's goals and objectives compatible with those of each limited partner?

Another precautionary note: To be fair in judging one accountant or lawyer versus another, you should acquire some knowledge of legal and accounting jargon before you go to your first interview. Otherwise, the first one or two interviewees will be at a disadvantage—in effect, they will be training you to understand the rest. By starting the interviewing process with some knowledge of the vocabulary, you will be able to give each interview equal weight.

Choosing a Broker

Limited partners probably don't need a real estate broker on their team of experts, since it is the general partner's responsibility to find the property and negotiate its purchase, management and sale. But I can say that the general partner's best source of properties is a reputable and compatible real estate broker. He (or

RELEASE OF LIABILITY

Date:________________

This release pertains to the following partnership interest and real property.

1. Name of partnership:________________
2. General partner(s):________________
3. Date partnership agreement was executed:________________
4. Address of property owned by partnership:

____

____

This agreement, made this ______day of ____________,1979 is between ________________________ (hereinafter referred to as "the general partner" acting on behalf of both the partnership and himself/herself individually) and ________________ (hereinafter referred to as "the limited partner.")

In consideration of the sum $______, the receipt of which is hereby acknowledged, the limited partner hereby releases both the partnership and all general and/or limited partners of said partnership from any and all claims, demands, actions, or suits of any kind.

It is the intention of the undersigned that this document constitutes a full release of all interest in the above referenced partnership and/or real property and a full release of liability on behalf of said partnership or any general or limited partner thereof arising from all present or future claims, known or unknown, foreseen or unforeseen, suspected or unsuspected.

____
initials of limited partner(s)

The limited partner(s) hereby waive any rights provided by section 1542 of the California Civil Code, which provides:

> "a general release does not extend to claims which the creditor does not know or suspect to exist in his favor at the time of executing the release, which if known by him must have materially affected his settlement with the debtor."

____
initials of limited partner(s)

Executed on date first above written.

________________ limited partner

________________ General partner

________________ limited partner

she) will find the property, tell you what the financing entails, and refer you to craftsmen, managers, and other professionals. Sometimes the broker will even find investors for you. Most general partners have at least two or three brokers looking for property for them or trying to find a buyer for property owned by the group.

As a buyer you get the broker's services free—the seller pays the commission. That means that the broker isn't working for you directly and you should understand that his motivation is to make a commission from the sale. Remember, your welfare is not his prime concern. I've become good friends with many of the brokers I've dealt with in my home state and in other states, and I trust their recommendations. But I always remember that a sale is their primary goal and pleasing me is secondary.

I don't recommend interviewing a real estate broker in the same way you interview an accountant or a lawyer. Here the most important considerations are what properties the broker can come up with and how fair and professional his services are. These are things you can judge only by seeing how a given broker actually performs. All you have to lose here is time, and you can control that to whatever extent you want.

Obviously you want a broker you can talk to, who is compatible, who is sensitive to your stated needs, and who doesn't try to overwhelm you with nonessential facts while holding back the information you really need. There are specialists in real estate brokering just as in other fields, so if you definitely want a multiple-unit apartment house, you should find a broker who handles that type of property. Some brokers specialize in commercial property, others in industrial property, residential income property, or single-family houses. Some have several specialties, but if you want an office-building investment, don't expect expert assistance from someone who usually deals in suburban houses.

The real estate business is complex, and in recent years has been especially unpredictable. The kind of broker you need is one who keeps up-to-date by attending professional meetings. He should have frequent contacts with experts on specific aspects of real estate—title-company people, maintenance and management professionals, lawyers, CPAs, and others involved in this active business. Because brokers are out in the field constantly, they know about properties that might not otherwise come to your attention.

To find a broker, review the classified ads of a local newspaper. The advertisements will provide you with the names of brokers who handle properties similar to the one you are interested in buying or selling. A telephone call begins the relationship and gives you a chance to make a preliminary evaluation.

After the phone call you'll probably receive some listings in the mail or in person. It's useful to go to the broker's office to see how well organized he is and how successful he appears to be.

A good broker can help you with your negotiations. Since he wants that commission from the sale, it is in his interest to bring the two parties together. The commission is his incentive to be innovative in order to close a transaction. He can make creative suggestions about methods of financing, ways to manage the property most profitably, and ways to package the group investment.

Below are things to look for in a real estate broker

(and you might also want to review Chapter 6, where the broker's listing sheet was discussed):

- Experience with the type or types of property you're considering for your group.
- Understanding of and responsiveness to your stated needs.
- Awareness of and respect for your time.
- Professional attitude.
- Knowledge of the area.
- Source for names of lawyers, CPAs, craftsmen, maintenance and management staff.

Choosing a Banker

Selecting a banker, the final member of your team of experts, usually begins with a visit to the manager of the bank with which you now do business. As a customer you've already established some relationship with the bank, whether or not you've been involved in borrowing.

You don't have to restrict yourself to this bank if you aren't satisfied it will provide the service—and money—you need. In a tight credit period it's harder to establish a new banking relationship, but it can be done. It's easier to get a banker's attention and cooperation when you are talking about establishing a credit line of $25,000 and up.

The best banker for a real estate group investor is one who understands real estate group investments. He should have the ability to be creative when necessary, instead of following guidelines designed for other kinds of investments—investments that don't require the same kind of open-mindedness that real estate does.

Your banker should know just what it is you need and want. He should be someone you can talk to confidentially and in a straightforward manner about your goals, why you are interested in this group investment, and what you hope to get from it. (When you visit the banker, take along your financial statement and copies of your latest income-tax returns.)

Although the bank manager or chief loan officer may not be an expert on real estate investments, he should be an expert on financing and credit, and have access to another member of the bank's staff who *is* knowledgeable about real estate. With that kind of backup a good banker will be able to guide you intelligently in financial matters.

It's a good idea to get to know your banker well. I find taking the banker to lunch gives us a chance to talk at length, free of distractions. In this kind of atmosphere you can learn how he feels about banking, how long he's been at his job, and what he thinks of the management and services of his bank. It's common to establish a relationship with a banker and then follow him to another bank if he changes jobs. That's how important the ties and communication can be between you and the banker. Your relationship is with him, really, not the bank.

Each state has its own banking regulations. Some permit branch banking; some do not. Generally a local bank is adequate as long as it is big enough to offer a full range of services and to provide the backup knowledge you will find useful from time to time.

One way I've dealt with a bank is by bringing in a

client of mine who needs short-term financing—say, $25,000 to $50,000 on a personal note. If you are a general partner, you will often need to work with your banker in this way. Someone who expresses interest in your group may have his money tied up. My banker can evaluate the situation quickly and come up with a fast personal loan for this potential limited partner. Everyone benefits. The bank makes money because the limited partner opens an account and starts a banking relationship with the bank. The limited partner gets the money he needs until his other assets are untangled. And the general partner has the satisfaction of providing the limited partner with good service and a good investment.

A Final Caveat

When dealing with experts, it's wise to keep in mind the other person's motivation. Just as a real estate broker is motivated by the sales commission, other experts have their own goals. Sometimes they overshadow your own—and there exists a potential conflict of interest. So although you should listen to the expert's point of view, you should always trust your own judgment in the final analysis. Although my team of experts is excellent, I remain alert to potential conflicts of interest. I also stay alert for errors. They *do* occur, even with the best of experts. That's why I started this chapter by saying the best protection is your own knowledge—and knowing what questions to ask. If something isn't absolutely clear to you, ask about it.

9 Looking Over the Prospectus

Since I'm not a lawyer, I can't give you legal advice. Each state has its own real estate laws. In my home state of California, for instance, there's a law commonly called the "10–25 ruling." The name refers to the fact that an offering qualifies as a *private* offering only if it is offered to no more than twenty-five people and is accepted by and distributed among no more than ten people. The people to whom the offer is made must have a preexisting personal or business relationship with the general partner, and the general partner must have business or financial experience and be financially able to protect the investors.

The Offering Memorandum

Your first encounter with a group investment is sure to be an offering memorandum, which is really a sales package that provides a basis for judging the value of the property. The more information you have, the better you and your experts can evaluate the investment.

An examination of each major point covered in the sample offering memorandum will show you what to expect in any such offering. If any of these points isn't covered, ask for clarification. Below is a typical offering memorandum, with comments interspersed. Names and addresses have been changed.

- You'll need a description of the investment. This doesn't have to appear at the beginning of the offering as long as it's included. Portsmouthe Development is an apartment complex, so along with information about each apartment and the common facilities (necessities such as parking, amenities such as pools and rec rooms), there are facts about the proximity of shopping and schools. An offering for a shopping center should tell you how much traffic passes the site and other facts pertinent to enticing shoppers to the center.

PORTSMOUTHE DEVELOPMENT

Portsmouthe Development is a newly formed limited partnership acquiring a 212-unit $9\frac{3}{4}$-acre, five-year-old complex on a street we'll call Beverly Drive, in Houston, Texas. The property is located approximately a few miles from downtown, two blocks from the intersection of two main highways. The area is characterized by single-family owner-occupied houses, town houses, and apartment projects.

There are twenty-two contemporary-design buildings of frame and brick veneer, 194 units are garden type, and 18 are town houses with 325 covered parking places. Most units are two-bedroom two-bath, ranging in size from 894 square feet to nearly 1,500 square feet. Features include refrigerator, electric range and exhaust hood, disposal, dishwasher, carpets and drapes, washer-dryer hookups in 165 units, marble vanities, beamed ceilings, and built-in bookcases; 26 units have wood-burning fireplaces. There are three air-conditioned, coin-operated laundry facilities, each of which has six washing machines and three dryers. The clubhouse is situated near the adult pool in a space over 1,000 square feet, with a "teen" room, pool table, and jukebox. A children's play area has heavy-duty recreation equipment, and there is also a "kiddie" pool. Connections for closed-circuit movies are available to tenants.

The property is in the Pine Branch school district and a public elementary school, public junior and senior high school, and a vocational center are a short distance from the property. Large regional shopping centers, small convenience shopping centers, churches of major denominations, restaurants, entertainment facilities, hospitals, fire, rescue squad, and police stations are all within five miles of the property.

There is an independent day-care center within two and one-half miles of the property. Also close by is a 44-acre public park which presently contains bikeways and an Olympic-size swimming pool. Contemplated or under construction are picnic areas, tennis courts, and athletic fields.

- The purchase terms for the property should be fully spelled out, including the price agreed on as well as the original price asked, the terms and conditions of the sale (such as mortgage payments and interest rates), the down payment, the amount of prepaid interest, and the points required to complete the sale. (Points are a one-time charge for initiating a loan. Usually they amount to 1 percent of the total face value of the loan.) Down payment, prepaid interest, and points are paid out of the limited partners' initial contributions.

CONTRACT OF SALE

The acquisition price is $4,680,000, originally listed at $5,244,000 with a down payment of $1,030,000, plus costs and prorations. We are acquiring the property subject to a wrap-around first mortgage of $2,978,561 and a second mortgage of $520,000, and a new purchase money third of $150,000. The first bears interest at 8⅝% with no prepayment penalty after 1985, due in 1994. The second is due in 1985 at 9½% per annum; no payments are due until December 1979. The third will be due in 1986, 10% interest, amortized 30 years.

The net rentable area is 234,338 square feet with expenses calculated at $433,525, or approximately $1.85 per foot. The investment should yield an initial net cash return of approximately 7% to investors, plus equity buildup, appreciation, and tax benefits.

- You should be told, in writing, about the planned management of the property: who will manage it and what kinds of reports you can expect as a limited partner.

Property management will be handled by the Gilbert Smith Co. in Houston with a staff of on-site personnel, and Jones Real Estate in Los Angeles. Cost for Smith Co. services are 3% of gross income less security deposits and are included in budgeted expenses. Management and syndication costs for Jones Real Estate will be 20% of profits as specified in the partnership agreement, item #12.

Escrow is scheduled to close on or about July 2, 1981. The minimum investment will be $100,000 and monies will be due no later than June 23, 1981. All funds will be deposited in an interest-bearing partnership account. Cashier's or certified checks should be made payable to PORTSMOUTHE DEVELOPMENT.

- It's helpful to have at least some information about the community, regardless of the type of property. The tone and style of the community will affect rentals, leases, future sales, and exchanges—and your income and profit.

ABOUT HOUSTON

Houston is known as a world center for research and production in medicine, energy, and space. It is the country's leading producer of petrochemicals and is entering a new coal age with four strip-mining units already in operation.

The Texas Medical Center is the largest in the world, LBJ Space Center is surrounded by more than 100,000 companies—a high-technology cluster second only to Los Angeles. Unemployment in Houston is lower than the national average, while industrial production and retail and building construction are considerably higher than the national average.

Between 2 and 3 million people live in Houston, the nation's fifth largest city and fastest-growing metropolitan area. Located in southeast Texas, 50 miles from the Gulf of Mexico, Houston enjoys a typically moderate-sunbelt climate averaging 59 degrees in winter and 82 degrees in summer.

Last year some 3 million visitors came to Houston to see the highlights: the Astrodome, Texas Medical Center, the famous River Oaks Country Club ($15,000 for initiation fees), Herman Park, and Houston's Main Street, the longest main street in the United States—36 miles of street and 18 miles of continuous business.

MANAGEMENT

JONES REAL ESTATE of Los Angeles and GILBERT SMITH CO. of Houston will be responsible for the ongoing management of the property. Their function will include the following:

1. Annual budget
2. Monthly reports
   a. Cash reconciliation
   b. Disbursements
   c. Payables
   d. Profit-and-loss statement
3. Quarterly report to investors
4. Annual reports
   a. Profit-and-loss statement
   b. Balance sheet
   c. Partnership tax return
   d. Complete set of books kept in accordance with generally accepted accounting practices

5. Payroll schedule (amended as needed)
6. Supervisor for administrative personnel
7. Supervisor for maintenance personnel
8. Total purchase control through field supervisors
9. Preventive maintenance program

• You also should know who the general partner or partners are. It isn't enough to know them personally. Their backgrounds and experience should be spelled out in writing.

GENERAL PARTNERS

SAM BARKER and JOHN JONES will be General Partners and conduct the business of the partnership from Empire Real Estate in Los Angeles and periodic on-site visits.

Sam Barker has successfully acquired and operated income-producing property for the past 15 years. Currently, she is a general partner in several large complexes in Austin, Texas, and several properties in southern California, and holds a master's degree in urban planning.

Sam Barker is a member of the Re-development Housing Task Force for the City of Los Angeles.

John Jones has until recently been responsible for the creation and operation of a multimillion-dollar credit-card company. As a licensed real estate salesperson, his unique understanding of the real estate marketplace has helped create many outstanding investments in California and Texas for himself and clients during the past several years. He has served as a consultant for the State of California and is currently consulting for VISA U.S.A. in San Francisco.

Mr. Jones is a private pilot and philatelist who is involved in several local charities and active politically in southern California, where he has lived for the past 35 years.

• The next three items, the apartment survey, first-year projection, and projection of tax flow, etc., give specifics about the value of the property (land and improvements), current income and expenses, and projected income and expenses. Carefully examine them. The more details you have, the better you can judge the value of the investment.

APARTMENT SURVEY

Total Number ______212______ Units
Age of "Subject Property" ______5½______ Years
Land Area ___9.7___ Acres ______422,532______ Sq.Ft.
Land Value (Total Estimated) ______$700,000______
Net Rentable Area ______234,338______ Sq.Ft.
Type of Metering ______Master______
Gross Potential Apartment Rent
(Including Miscellaneous Income) ______$893,973______
Gross Multiplier
(Sales Price Divided by Gross Rent) ______5⅓X______
Equity (% of Sales Price) ______22______
Approximate Net Cash Flow
Return to Investors ______7______ %
Operating Expenses (% of Gross) ______48______
Operating Expenses (per Sq.Ft.) ___$1.85___
Debt Service (% of Gross) ______38.5______ %
Price per Unit ______$22,066______
Price per Rentable Sq.Ft. ______$19.96______
Average Area Occupancy
as of April 1979 ______95______ %

Current "Subject Property" Occupancy 99 %
Break-even Occupancy 86.6 %
Average Area Rent $345
Average Rent $344
Average Rent Per Sq.Ft. $.31
Length of Lease 6-12 Months

FIRST-YEAR PROJECTION

PORTSMOUTHE DEVELOPMENT—There are 212 units, the majority are two-bedroom/two-baths, with some three-bedroom/two-baths, and four-bedroom/two-bath units. Most apartments have utility rooms and the town houses include fireplaces. There is over 234,000 square feet of rentable space on 9¾ acres in Houston, Texas. The price was $4,680,000 with $1,030,000 down plus costs and prorations.

INCOME

Current street rents ($.31 per square foot)	$876,000
Laundry, vending, and miscellaneous income	17,973
Vacancy at 3½% (only one vacancy as of 4/20/79)	(30,660)
Net Income	$863,313

DEBT SERVICE

1st: $2,978,561.79 at 8⅝% amortized 30 years due 1994	$(290,040)
2nd: $400,000 at 9½% plus accrued interest; $520,000 if no payment made until 12/15/79 due 1984—interest only	(38,000)

3rd: $150,000 at 10% amortized 30 years due 1986	(15,795)
Debt Service	$(343,835)

EXPENSES

Approximately $1.85 per square foot: electric $116,970; water $13,032; gas $9,749; taxes $80,004; and other expenses at $.90 per square foot	(433,525)
Cash Flow	$85,953

DISTRIBUTIONS

General Partners	$17,191
Limited Partners	$68,762

Approximately 7% net return to limited partners after all costs, management, and syndication fees.

PROJECTION OF CASH FLOW, TAX BENEFITS, AND RETURN ON INVESTMENT INITIAL YEAR OF ACQUISITION

CASH FLOW

EFFECTIVE GROSS REVENUE

Scheduled Gross Rent—$.31 per square foot	$876,000
Less vacancy factor—3½%	(30,660)
Laundry and vending income	17,973
Total Effective Gross Revenue	863,313

OPERATING EXPENSES

Electric, $116,970; water $13,032; Gas $9,749; taxes, $80,004; other $213,770	433,525
	429,788

NET OPERATING INCOME				
DEBT SERVICE	*Interest*	*Principal*	*Total*	
First trust deed, $2,978,562	$285,763	$4,277	$290,040	
Second trust deed, $400,000	38,000	—	38,000	
Third trust deed, $150,000	14,961	834	15,795	
Total Debt Service	$338,724	$5,111	$343,835	(343,835)
				85,953

NET CASH FLOW

TAX BENEFITS

Net operating income	$429,789	
Less interest expense (above)	(338,724)	
Less depreciation—30-year building life, 85% allocation of purchase cost to building, 10% salvage	(119,280)	
Taxable (loss)	$(28,216)	
NET TAX BENEFITS (assuming 50% taxpayer)		14,108
PRINCIPAL REDUCTION RE UNDERLYING DEBT (above)		5,111
TOTAL RETURN ON INVESTMENT		$105,172

• The next section of the offering memorandum tells what is expected of the limited partners. This includes a description of the gross amount of cash being raised in the offering, the price per unit, the number of units being sold, and the minimum investment required of each partner. Also included: a description of the compensation and profits due the general partner and a statement about when such compensation and profits are to be paid. Tax factors, tax risks, and a lawyer's opinion on taxation of the partnership and tax aspects of the offering are valuable elements. The offering should invite the prospective limited partners (and their experts) to examine all the documents concerning the property's acquisition and the limited partnership itself.

RISK FACTORS

Organization of Limited Partnership

The proposed Partnership will be a Limited Partnership and the Limited Partners of such a Partnership will be subject to the restrictions of the agreement. While, under existing laws, this form of organization makes possible more favorable income-tax consequences for investors than would be the case under a corporate form of organization, it should be understood that investors in a Limited Partnership do not have all the rights, remedies, procedures, protections, and guarantees which are possessed by the shareholders of a corporation. For instance, the Limited Partners will have no right to manage or control the Partnership or to vote on any matters concerning the Partnership except termination of the Partnership and amendments to the agreement.

Income Taxes
Certain income tax advantages are projected to be realized from the investment. No assurance is given that any tax deductions or other advantages that may be claimed will not be disallowed by the tax authorities, nor is there any guarantee that the tax laws or regulations or the interpretation of existing or new laws will not change so as to deprive the investors of any tax benefits projected herein.

Ability to Meet Cash Distributions
The Partnership's ability to meet its cash obligations as they become due and payable will depend upon such factors, among others, as rate of occupancy and the rental schedule which can be sustained and the level of expenditures required for the operation of said property. Accordingly, the Partnership's ability to meet its cash obligations and the possibility of appreciation in value of the property may be adversely affected by factors which are beyond the control of the General Partner, including local and general economic conditions, the supply of and demand for property, which may render the sale or refinancing of the property difficult or unattractive. In addition, any decrease in gross rentals received by the Partnership from the property may disproportionately reduce, and possibly eliminate, the amount of cash available for distribution to its Limited Partners, since most operating expenses of the Partnership, including interest on borrowed funds, operating expenses of the property, and property taxes, remain relatively constant and must be met regardless of the level of gross income.

Regulation of Partnership
The Limited Partnership interest will not be registered with the Securities and Exchange Commission. The

General Partners are relying on an exemption from registration for the sale of securities which do not involve a public offering. Accordingly, each purchaser will be required to execute a Participation Agreement containing a representation that his purchase is not being made with any present intent to resell, distribute, or in any way transfer or dispose of his interest in the Partnership.

The Limited Partnership is being formed pursuant to the Uniform Limited Partnership Act of the State of California, as amended:

> The offer or sale of partnership interests to limited partners pursuant to this limited partnership agreement, have not been registered with the Securities and Exchange Commission under the Securities Act of 1933, as amended, nor have the offer or the sale of such interests been qualified with the Commissioner of Corporations of the State of California.

This is not a prospectus nor should it be considered as the offer of any securities for sale or the solicitation of or offer to buy securities. The Limited Partnership interests herein described are being offered on a selected private basis to a limited number (which shall not exceed 25) of sophisticated investors of adequate means, and sales will be consummated to not more than 10 of such investors.

Fiduciary Responsibility of the General Partner

The General Partner is accountable to the Partnership as a fiduciary, which means he is required to exercise good faith and integrity in dealings with respect to Partnership affairs. This is in addition to the duties, obligations, and limitations of the General Partner as set forth in the agreement of Limited Partnership. Each Limited Partner, or his authorized representative, may inspect the books and records at any time during normal business hours.

Disclaimer

This memorandum is a projection only and as such should be considered. There are no warranties or implications that this is a true picture and nothing written here should be construed as a guarantee of return.

Estimates, projections, and opinions which are included in this memorandum should not be interpreted as statements of fact. This memorandum is not necessarily complete.

The above information contained herein has been received from the owner and his agent and is deemed to be accurate and reliable. However, this memorandum is subject to errors, omission, correction, change, prior sale, or WITHDRAWAL without notice.

No person is authorized to give any information or to make any representation not contained in this memorandum. Any information or representation not contained herein must not be relied upon as having been authorized by the Partnership or the General Partner.

All of these facts are based upon projections as to the market conditions and there is no way we can foresee the future.

Note: The offering memorandum continues with details about the gross amount of cash raised in the offering, the price per unit, the minimum investment per person, the number of units being sold, the compensation due the general partners, an analysis of tax factors and tax risks, a summary of the lawyer's opinion on taxation of the partnership and tax aspects of the offering, and an invitation to the limited partners to examine all documents connected with the purchase and the agreement.

- It's helpful if the offering memorandum includes a map of the location of the property and photographs or renderings of the property. Floor plans also help you to visualize the potential purchase.

The Participation Agreement

When you've satisfied yourself that you want to be part of the investment group, it's time to fill out a participation agreement. This is the first legal document the limited partners sign *before* investing.

Many states require such an agreement to protect investors. It should establish that the person entering the deal is substantial and sophisticated, and that he or she understands that any investment is a risk and therefore has ample resources if this investment fails. In days past people sometimes put all their worldly goods into a project. If it failed, they were left penniless.

A sample participation agreement may be found in Appendix C.

The Certificate of Limited Partnership

In some states (California among them) limited partners must be validated by the filing of a certificate of limited partnership for recording in the county where the property is located *and* the county where the general partner's principal business is located. Copies that have been dated and stamped by the county recorder are mailed to the general partners, who in turn mail copies to the limited partners.

This certificate summarizes the agreement of the parties and includes the names and residence addresses of each partner (general and limited), the amount of money each contributes, provisions for shares of profits, and provisions for the rights of all parties.

The Limited-Partnership Agreement

The heart of the whole group partnership is the limited-partnership agreement. It and its exhibits are what make the group legal.

The document need not be complicated. In fact, it should be written clearly and concisely. You'll want your lawyer and accountant to review it, of course, but it should also be understandable to you. After all, you are the person who is putting up the money. You have the most to gain and the most to lose.

Characteristics of a Corporation

Before a group real estate investment can qualify for the tax benefits, it must fail a test—the test of whether it is a corporation. Under current federal tax laws a limited partnership has to lack at least two of the four characteristics of a corporation. It isn't hard to qualify as a limited partnership, but the vital points must be covered in the agreement. In their book, *Real Estate Limited Partnership,** authors Theodore S. Lynn, Harry F. Goldberg, and Daniel S. Abrams describe the four characteristics of a corporation, two of which must be lacking to qualify for a limited partnership.

1. A corporation has a *continuity of life.* Even if its officers die, go bankrupt, retire, become insane, resign, or are expelled, the corporation lives on. A group can fail the test of continuity of life by providing for automatic dissolution if the general partner dies, goes bankrupt, retires, becomes insane, resigns, or is booted out. A new partnership would then have to be formed to protect and continue the investment.
2. A corporation has *centralized management.* A partnership usually passes this test.
3. A corporation has *limited liability.* The limited partnership agreement can fail this test by making the general partner personally liable for the debts or claims against the group. This means the general partner must have sufficient assets to meet such debts or claims. It also means the general partner has

*Published by John Wiley & Sons, Inc., New York.

to be legitimately in charge—he can't be acting as an agent for the limited partners, accountable to the limited partners' orders.

4. A corporation has *free transferability of shares.* The partnership can fail this test by providing that no partner can transfer his share without the written consent of the general partner. In other words, the partnership agreement must state that there is no free transferability of interests.

Now it's time to dig yourself out from under that pile of paperwork and negotiate to close the deal.

10 The Art of Negotiating: Closing the Deal

Assembling a group, locating the right property, and finding the purchase money are all crucial steps in putting a syndication together, but negotiating is often much more difficult. The general partner negotiates to buy the property and to sell or exchange it later, but limited partners should understand what the process entails. Knowing the general partner's skill at the negotiating table can be the deciding factor in choosing one with whom to invest.

The single purpose of any negotiation is to obtain the best possible deal for the group; the general partner's ability to get the most favorable terms and conditions is the key to the successful conclusion of the deal. The other party to the transaction has a different point of view, of course. In any negotiation the person on the other side of the table—the seller of the property your group wants or a potential buyer—also wants the best possible deal for himself.

Later in this chapter I'll tell you about specific items that can be negotiated, but first let's look at some of the techniques of negotiating—the art of closing the deal satisfactorily.

The general partner doesn't always have to do the actual negotiating. That responsibility can be assigned to a lawyer, an accountant, or another third party. A general partner would be derelict, however, if he wasn't aware of all stages of the negotiations. Even if he is only quietly watching, he should be there with eyes and ears open. The reason a third party may do the actual negotiating is that sometimes the person who can do the best job is not the general partner but someone who has that special negotiating skill, without necessarily having the interest and/or skills to be a general partner. In this case negotiating becomes a team effort.

Unfortunately it's impossible to give a definitive description of a good negotiator. All kinds of people are effective, from the most abrasive to the most gentle and disarming. Good negotiators draw on their personal strengths and downplay their weaknesses. How they operate depends on what those strengths are. Sometimes, too, the negotiator has to change his style to suit the occasion. One time, his aggressive, strong position wins out; the next time, he finds a low-key approach is more successful.

The negotiator's first step is to establish the group's investment goals. These are usually based on one or more of four basic points:

1. The group's need for spendable income and/or equity buildup.
2. The group's need for a safe, secure investment.
3. The group's need for tax benefits to shelter participants' regular income.
4. The group's need to sell the property at a high profit.

Groups seek a blend of these goals, and the ideal property offers some cash flow, some safety, some tax benefits, and some growth in value. But it's up to the negotiator to stress the points most important to the specific group of investors.

If your group is primarily after tax benefits, then the negotiator will hold out for as large a mortgage as possible, since that provides the greatest tax deductions. If the principal goal is safety and low risk, the negotiator might consider an all-cash purchase. If your group wants maximum spendable income from a purchased property, the negotiator will know he has some leverage because the property that usually gives the best yield is in a marginal area, where prices are lower but properties are harder to sell. (When your group attempts to sell such a property later, the negotiator for your group must realize the shoe is now on the other foot.)

Before sitting down to negotiate specific points, the

general partner and his support team should reevaluate the broker's sheet on the prospective purchase. Then the general partner makes an offer. The offer should not establish a bottom price—it is a mistake to do this too early in the talks—and should provide flexible terms.

To give you an idea of just how extensive negotiations—and the number of topics negotiated—can be, it is not unusual for closing statements on the sale of larger properties to have a two-inch-high pile of legal documents setting out terms and conditions. Most negotiations are not that elaborate, of course, but they can get very detailed and, yes, tedious. Stay with it if the deal is worth it, however.

Valuable Negotiating Techniques

- Be prepared for the negotiating. Understand yourself, your motivation, your goals, and your bottom-line limits and expectations.
- It helps to put yourself in the other person's shoes. Once you understand his position, you might be able to determine where you're likely to gain some flexibility. The three big areas for deliberations are price, terms, and conditions. If you know your opponent's point of view and motivation, you might be able to predict where the flexibility lies. Price isn't always the motivation for selling, for example.
- Begin with high expectations and a low price if you're buying—and with high expectations and a high price if you're selling. But be sufficiently rea-

sonable to avoid having the other party ignore your offer as insincere.

- Don't be afraid to use a little gamesmanship. For example, the old good guy/bad guy routine still works at times. That is, go into face-to-face negotiations with a partner who plays the good guy, willing to yield and be nice, while you take a tough, unyielding position (or vice versa). With this type of gamesmanship (even if the other side knows exactly what you're up to or thinks it does) you have the leeway to move in whatever direction appears appropriate at the moment. The good guy can do some bending while the bad guy takes more wooing.
- You should know what concessions you are willing to make before you go into negotiations. Snap decisions can be risky and costly. A concession of any significant point should be carefully considered before it's made. If you haven't prepared yourself on some aspect of the purchase, postpone discussing it until the next session.
- When you make concessions, it helps to explain them to the other party. That gives him some idea of your objectives. By the same token, you should be prepared to explain why you can't concede some points.
- It's helpful to control the agenda of the negotiations meeting and to direct the negotiating. You might want to set up the order of topics so that your stronger arguments come first (or last).
- Silence is an effective tool. The person listening often actually controls the situation; the one who needs to talk to fill a void will often disclose information useful to the other side.
- The most effective negotiators are even-handed

and objective (or appear to be), well prepared (with a comprehensive and orderly presentation of the offer), and insightful. They listen to the other party express his needs, conserve time and move forward, and avoid asking such questions as "Is this agreeable?" They assume that it *is* agreeable unless the other side objects.

- Creative thinking includes the ability and willingness to explore alternative steps. If the other side is being competitive, this might not work. But if you believe the other party is trying to be cooperative by suggesting an alternative, it helps to hear him out with an open mind.
- Keep an eye on the nonverbal communications. If the other negotiator is giving body-language signs of stress or frustration or interest or defensiveness, you should be aware of them and consider how they can serve your group's best interests.
- Realize that the other person is watching your nonverbal communications, too.
- Avoid getting caught in negotiation traps that put you on the defensive. The other party might complain about some insignificant calculation error or be critical of your being five minutes late. Just make a simple apology and move on. Don't play his game.
- Acknowledge the other negotiator's skills with genuine warmth if he's come to the meeting well prepared. Then, having made the acknowledgment, move into the discussion of the larger issues.
- Acknowledge the other negotiator's *non*skills if he tries to snow you with superfluous facts and figures. You can do this by asking for a brief summary of his position.

Games Negotiators Play

There are many roles played by people negotiating for a property. Below are some examples:

Mister Oblivious, who glides over a concession you've just made, acting as though it is his by divine right instead of acknowledging that it is, in fact, a concession. If this happens, emphasize that it *is* a concession and explain why you are making it. This is one reason that I suggest you be well prepared.

Madam Generosity, who offers you a crumb as if it were a seven-tier cake just so she can get a big concession from you. Your response to that one is simple: Let her know it's a crumb, not a cake, and don't make *your* concession unless she makes an equally big one.

Mister Lower Echelon, who says he doesn't have the authority to speak for the buyer/seller, or can't sign anything, or can't make a decision without the "big guy's" approval. Simply state that you cannot negotiate with him until he obtains more authority, and if he can't get the authority, you want someone across the table from you who can.

Miss Naive, who plays dumb to get your sympathy. It usually takes the form of putting herself or someone else down as a defenseless character in need of your solicitous help and kindness. Your response should be silence. Just don't play.

Mister Yawn, who acts uninterested or bored while you're making your point. You may think he's just rude, but this behavior could be a ploy to undermine your confidence. Again, the clever response is to refuse to play the game. If he goes too far, tell him he seems rather tired today and perhaps you ought to get together another time when he is rested enough to concentrate on negotiations. This is one time that putting *him* on the defensive is fair.

Mister Putdown, who suggests that negotiations would go much better if you weren't so unfair/unprepared/uncompromising. Respond with a smile and silence.

Miss Yesbut, who agrees with everything you say but adds the qualifier "yes, but" so that in fact all your offers are rejected except the one or ones she wants. It's a way of looking cooperative without *being* cooperative, and it is best to ignore it.

The important thing is always to know when a game is being played, and to turn it to your advantage. Don't let yourself be a pawn in the negotiations of others, either, as I once was with a syndicator-developer in Texas.

His creditors were about to foreclose, I was told, and he needed a buyer. His lawyer called my lawyer, who called me. We met, I got an idea of the figures involved, and we agreed to fly to Texas together the next morning.

When we got to his attorney's office in Texas, I learned that the lawyers there were representing not only him but also the bank from which he had borrowed the money. I began to suspect that I had been brought along to enhance his credibility with the bank, that the people holding the mortgage had already decided to take over the property and I was there only in case the negotiation fell through.

"Am I a backup?" I asked him.

"Would I do that to you?" he said. You can guess the answer to that one.

By and large, I've had good experiences in real estate. There are a few people like the fellow I've just described, but I've found that most people can be trusted on a handshake.

Negotiation Limits

Before we explore the specific items that can be negotiated, it's appropriate to look at some negotiation limits. The primary limits are unique to each group: They are imposed by its goals and objectives. For a group that relies on spendable income, the negotiator must not set up an agreement that negates or minimizes that income. For a group dependent on a tax shelter, the limits again are obvious.

There is another limit, which is illustrated by the famous "pie" chart for an apartment-house investment:

The most important limit is that the cost of the mortgage should almost never exceed half the income. If it does, the balance will be weighted to the detriment of the group. I say *almost* never because there is an exception. If the rents for the property you're considering are below the market level and you have the capital to tide you over until rent increases make up for the imbalance, buy it. Just be sure first that you will be able to adjust the rents upward.

Another limit is that the total expenses should not exceed 40 to 45 percent of the income. For a given month or two that rule might not hold, but it's a good general limit when you're considering possible concessions for negotiations.

Also critical is that the buyer should know, without

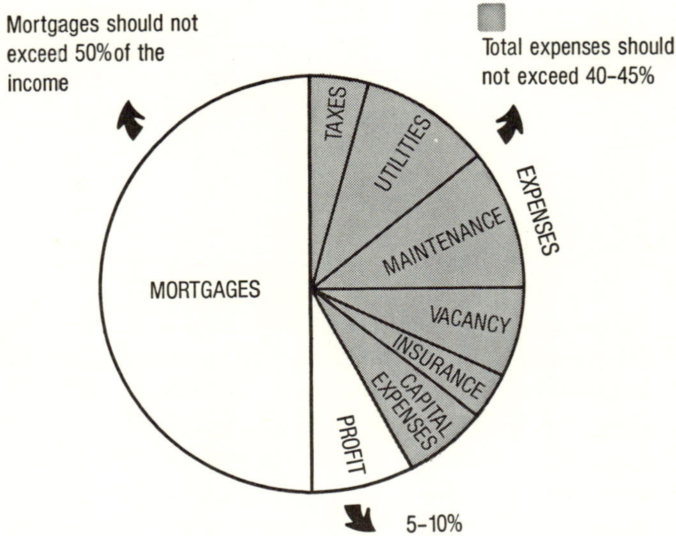

question or doubt, the present income from the property, what it could realistically be in the near future, and what expenses are pressing as well as what repairs and changes might be needed later that would cause additional expense. Since vacancies are part of the expense picture, the negotiator needs to know what can be expected here, too.

All this information is obtained through a thorough study of the manager's and others' records of the property and through a site analysis conducted independently by the general partners and their representatives. The site analysis should include a visit to the local planning department; a city's master plan can turn up some interesting and/or disheartening facts.

Use your experts, with their special knowledge of the area. Again, it's necessary to be alert to a possible conflict of interest—the expert you're depending on might have something to gain from the sale or purchase.

Negotiating Areas

Generally speaking, all negotiations are concerned with price, terms, and conditions. But these three major categories encompass many subjects. Thinking in subgroups of money and financing, building and grounds, and legal documents can help you sort out the points you'll need to cover as a negotiator.

1. Money and financing. This area is the biggest and includes the most critical points. At the top of the list is the selling price, but in saying that I want to stress that price isn't always the decisive factor. If the terms are good, a higher price may be acceptable. Or the opposite may be true: The price is fine but the terms are too steep.

It is accurate to say that the selling price is always negotiable in one way or another. Even if a seller absolutely refuses to consider any sum lower than the asking price, you might be able to wring from him some concessions that amount to a reduction in price. One example is getting the seller to agree to pay all the closing costs—costs that are normally paid in part by the buyer. This in effect reduces the actual price you are paying for the property. The reverse is also true: If your group is selling and the buyer refuses to move on price, you might be able to get him to pay all closing costs.

Financing terms are the second most important negotiating point, closely related to the selling price. Willingness to create a wrap-around mortgage—an all-inclusive trust deed—that gives the buyer a lower-than-market mortgage interest rate is another form of effectively reducing the selling price of a property

The due date for a deed of trust or the percentage points that a seller can give as an incentive can be a big negotiating point. For the seller who is carrying back a second deed of trust, a note for the shortest possible time is usually preferable. For the buyer the opposite point of view prevails: He usually wants a longer time so he can be assured of raising sufficient cash for the balloon payment (usually due in two to five years). The seller wants the highest rate possible; the buyer wants the lowest. These are areas for negotiation.

A negotiator for a group buying real estate with a wrap-around or second mortgage should be aware that the balloon payment can put the group in a highly vulnerable position if it comes due too soon. It can force a sale at a time that is not best for investors' interests or compel the general partner to go to the limited partners for more cash. If you're the general partner, you may be obligated to come up with that cash yourself if the limited partners are unable or unwilling to do so.

Years ago this payment wasn't a problem because investors could always count on refinancing the second mortgage when the balloon payment came due. But today you cannot count on refinancing, even at high interest rates, and there's no sign that the money market will become stable in the near future.

Another important part of the money and financing aspect of negotiations is the cash down payment. Although the amount is governed in part by the availability of financing, including wrap-around mortgage financing, it remains a point for discussion and possible compromise. A group might be willing to make a higher down payment in return for, say, longer terms on the second mortgage or splitting a down payment over a year or two.

Another money matter is the amount of good-faith or earnest money that has to be deposited to hold the property during negotiations. As a buyer you'll want this figure to be as low as possible, partly because you want to keep the loss down in case the deal falls through and partly because negotiations can sometimes take longer than expected and you don't want your money tied up for that time. In any event, you should insist on being paid interest on the good-faith deposit. (Again, the seller will take the opposite point of view in most instances.)

The time of closing is in the money-and-financing category because it's then that the money to complete the transaction comes due. Whether you want to accelerate or delay the closing depends on where your group stands—whether it has the money and is ready to close or needs additional time to get the cash together for a purchase. Sellers generally want to close as soon as possible; buyers generally want more time unless they're making an exchange or want an end-of-the-year tax benefit.

One of the factors that affect the closing date is who pays what closing costs. Commonly, property taxes and other annual fees are prorated, with the buyer paying the amount left over after the closing date. This, too, is negotiable, however.

Your attorney or accountant can guide you in determining how one closing date or another will affect the group, including its tax benefits. What may seem like a good negotiating point may turn out to be a mistake if it adversely affects the tax deductions of the group you represent.

Still another consideration is who will pay any prepayment penalties attached to premature payment of the mortgage. Some states have banned prepayment penalties, but others have not. Check with your lawyer to determine the laws in the state where the property is bought or sold.

Real estate brokers will grimace when they read this, but I've found that one of the most flexible negotiating points of all is the broker's commission. Sometimes the question of who pays the commission, and how, can be the difference between making or losing a sale.

Normally the seller pays the commission at the time the transaction is formally closed. But that practice isn't carved in granite. The buyer and seller can agree to share payment of the commission, or the broker can agree to take a part of the property, a second or third mortgage, in lieu of his commission. Naturally, most brokers prefer their commission in cash. After all, they have usually worked for it and they, too, have bills to pay. But frequently I have seen brokers make adjustments. I've known them to agree to time payments or even to cut their commissions. Such adjustments are fairly common and are a viable point for negotiation. Here, of course, the agreement extends beyond the representatives of the buyer and seller. The broker is a necessary party.

Income and expense information is also a point for negotiation, for including the provision of this information in the terms of the sales contract may be the only way the buyer can be sure of getting the true figures. You could choose to trust the seller and accept what he gives you, but you would be taking a chance because so often obscure or incorrect information appears on the broker's sheets and other preliminary-data sheets.

I've seen sellers put down property-tax figures that are two or three years old, or avoid mentioning projected or proposed increases in taxes or utility costs. As the general partner for a group you have to be especially wary of these devices. More than your own name, reputation, and money are at stake because you also represent your limited partners.

My negotiations usually include a provision for a certified rent roll with the names of each tenant, the monthly rental fees, the expiration date of each lease, the amounts of prepaid and delinquent rent, a statement that there are no unperformed obligations of the landlord not embodied in the written lease, and the amount of each tenant's deposit (for security, say, or a pet). The roll also should provide that the seller will pay the buyer an amount equal to the deposits at the time of closing and that any disputes that arise with tenants during the escrow or sales period are the responsibility of the seller. I also include provisions for an audit by my CPA of the expense records of the property.

Another element in the money and financing category is the exchanging of property—with or without exchanging money. In negotiations there may be some flexibility in deciding the size of one property's equity compared to another's.

2. Buildings and Grounds. This next body of considerations for negotiating involves building and grounds conditions.

An easement is an agreement allowing one person to use the property of another, and it might be a factor in deciding to purchase a property. Your group might want to create an easement and agree to the purchase only if it *is* created. An encroachment is an improvement—of a building or part of a building—that extends beyond one property's line onto the property of another.

Both easements and encroachments are items that should be mentioned in the sales agreement. The negotiator can ask that the seller indemnify his group against any such easements or encroachments.

A soil report is another necessity. I've seen ground that looked terrific for a development, but the soil report showed it couldn't be built on.

You'll also want to be sure that zoning is appropriate and that your seller guarantees that no zoning violations exist on the land being sold. I once looked at a reasonably priced property with four apartment buildings on it. Then I learned on my own that it was zoned for only two apartment buildings. The broker hadn't checked this. I pulled out, hoping that no one else would get caught buying something he might well have to tear down. Negotiate for this kind of protection.

Another item of protection: Have the seller indemnify you against building-permit violations. These are more frequent than you might guess because people often add rooms or alter electrical wiring or do other construction without obtaining the necessary permits. If you buy a property with these violations, the violations become your problem and can turn into a big headache—especially when you try to resell.

An item that is not one for indemnification but can

be used for flexibility in settling on a price is the personal property that does or does not come with a building. In an apartment complex this might include stoves, refrigerators, indoor and outdoor furniture, recreation equipment, and pool and other maintenance materials. You need an inventory of the items and to be safe, take it yourself.

You can also use personal property as a sales tool. As a seller you might want to include more to make the sale more appealing. As a buyer you may suggest excluding the personal property—especially if it's in poor or mediocre condition—to reduce the selling price.

The final point to consider in building and grounds condition is the physical condition of the property and improvements. Most properties should be inspected by both the general partner and independent experts, who test out everything from termites to plumbing to roofing to structural soundness to the physical appearance of each room. I've seen cannibalized apartments that weren't noticed until the new owners took over. Everything removable was gone, including furnaces and light fixtures. They'd all been used to repair other apartments. If your inspection turns up stripped apartments, your negotiations should provide that the seller either fixes them up or gives you an allowance for the repairs plus vacancy during the time it takes to repair them.

Occasionally a property looks like a worthwhile purchase "as is." These cases are rare, but they do occur. Before you go into negotiations on such a property, hire some knowledgeable people to poke around the place so you'll understand just what "as is" means. Sometimes a seller is willing to let a place go at a good price rather than spend the time and money to fix it up. If you agree to a purchase "as is," you should be absolutely certain that the price is as good as you think it is.

3. Legal documents. Paperwork again. If there are leases, you'll need copies. If the leases lock you into too-low rents for a long time, that's a negotiable point when settling on the price. Every new buyer wants to raise rents to produce more income. With long-term leases you don't have that option.

Request a preliminary title report before you start negotiations so you know you are negotiating with the true owners. Also ask for a final title policy. Who pays for that might be the subject of negotiations.

Often people don't pay much attention to insurance policies or outstanding service contracts during negotiations, but they, too, can be used. A seller can sweeten the transaction by agreeing to keep such policies and contracts in effect during the transition period, while the new owners are settling in. Or a buyer can agree to cancel all contracts and policies because he can do as well or better by bringing in new people—or his own trusted resources. Some sellers want to keep the contractors happy because they use them elsewhere. They might concede on some other point if the buyer will agree to use the same contractors and insurer for a given period.

One other important point is the issue of contingencies. A contingency agreement is an agreement to do something contingent upon something else first happening.

An example of this is an agreement to sell a property contingent upon the seller finding an acceptable exchange. I was once a third party, willing to buy the seller's shopping center as soon as the exchange was found and concluded. I signed the sales agreement, with this contingency, and the seller had my earnest-money deposit. This was in the days before I got smart enough to require interest on a deposit. Not only was my money tied up while the seller was looking for the exchange property; it wasn't even earning simple interest. The money had been in limbo for more than a year when the seller backed out because he couldn't find a suitable exchange. He had that right—the sale was contingent upon the exchange, and the exchange never occurred.

Contingency agreements should in general, be avoided. They are often a part of negotiations, however. In a typical contingency agreement made by a seller, he agrees to sell you his property contingent upon getting 10 percent financing. Then the loan doesn't come through. You've tied your property and the buyer can back out because you weren't able to negotiate the loan. This is the kind of contingency agreement to avoid. But if the other side offers to make a contingency agreement advantageous to you, do so.

Not all contingency agreements, of course, are bad. Some are valid, such as an agreement "contingent upon inspection of the property" or "contingent upon inspection of the books."

Before getting involved in negotiations, it might be helpful to check your memory of the key points involved in closing a real estate transaction:

1. List at least three negotiable points that deal with

the money and financing aspects of purchasing or selling a property:

____

____

____

2. List at least three negotiable points that deal with the building and grounds conditions of purchasing or selling a property:

____

____

____

3. List at least three negotiable points that deal with the legal documents connected with purchasing or selling a property:

____

____

____

Answers: 1—sales price, exchanges, trades, lease options, cash down payments, good-faith or earnest-money deposits, the methods, terms, and conditions of financing, broker commissions, closing time, closing costs, income and expense information; *2*—easements, encroachments, repairs, soil reports, personal property, surveys, zoning, building permits, known and unknown defects; *3*—leases, insurance, title policies, outstanding contracts.

11 Managing Management

Management of the property is the next vital phase after the deal is closed. Competent management is crucial because it may ultimately determine if a group makes or loses money. Although limited partners don't get involved in management, they should understand it.

When you start managing, you have two basic things to work with: income and expenses. Everything left over from income after expenses is profit, and how you handle income and expenses will largely determine how much profit you make.

There's one goal for income: Raise it. There's another for expenses: Reduce them. Neither goal may be attainable at first, but you should have figured out the probabilities before you bought the property and have kept them in mind while negotiating the price and the terms of sale.

Perhaps you will need to make some expenditures—for instance, on painting or major repairs—before you can increase income. But the day will arrive when you can consider raising rents. It may be just after you take over the property, but it can take time if rent-control laws are in effect, if tenants have leases, if the property is already rented up to or beyond fair market prices, or if extensive repairs are needed.

Some of the questions you considered when you first thought about buying the property are relevant before you try to increase income: Are rentals at fair market value, at least equal to comparable rentals in the area? Should you raise everyone's rent at once? Should you pass on utility costs? Are there other untapped sources of additional income, such as laundry machines, vending machines, or recreation-room games?

No one likes to have his rent increased, but if you are fair, you will probably be able to keep most tenants without too much distress. (One guide to what's fair is the "pie" on p. 164.)

Who Should Manage?

One major expense of managing an apartment building can be the management itself. I suggest that single dwellings or those with six or fewer units be managed by one of the general partners or by someone else with a vested interest in the property's good management.

An on-site manager is enough for a building with seven to thirty units. That manager should report directly to the general partner.

For buildings with thirty or more units, professional property-management firms are a wise choice. They select and supervise the on-site manager and assume responsibility for the day-to-day management of the property. Still, the general partner must keep in touch with and oversee the management firm.

A good resident manager is a tremendous bonus. I've known the whole range of types, from excellent to poor. I've also seen what happens when a manager is in conflict with the tenants. The following story involved a friend, but anyone can have problems with a manager.

The property was a thirty-six-unit apartment complex, mostly two-bedroom units, for middle-income working people, some with children and some without. Everyone got along well. Then the managers decided to move to the country and my friend interviewed a number of potential new managers. One couple came highly recommended and she hired them.

A few months later, the vandalism began. The final straw was when crankcase oil was found in the swimming pool. My friend, the general partner for the partnership that owned the property, talked with the tenants to find out what was going on. She soon learned.

The resident managers, who had given every appearance of being cooperative and capable, had set themselves up as judge and jury for all the tenants, especially those with children. A child running was cause for harsh reprimands and threats of eviction. Payment of rent a day or two late was met with snarling asides, even if the tenant was usually prompt and had merely been out of town on the first of the month.

There were many such stories. Most tenants simply ignored this treatment, but some had reacted with equal or greater hostility. When the resident managers were dismissed, the vandalism ended quickly.

When you buy a new property, meet with the present on-site manager if there is one. You'll be fortunate if he or she is competent and willing to stay on, for the continuity will be soothing to the tenants, who are probably worried that their rent will be going up soon because of the change in owners.

Find out if the manager is willing to accept the fact that there will be rent increases at some time in the future. Some managers feel more loyalty to the tenants than to the owners. This isn't too surprising, since the tenants are their neighbors. Proper perspective is necessary, however, for the manager will, after all, be your employee and be paid by you.

The first way to test a manager is with a phone call. Is the response to your call friendly, efficient, and businesslike? Or is it offhand—or nonexistent because the manager is never there to answer the phone? A poor response is a problem you will have to handle.

Below is a checklist of points to consider if you as a general partner need to hire a resident manager:

- Has the manager had any professional training useful in property management, such as courses in bookkeeping and managing property?
- Is he the right person for the property? (The

person who is ideal for an older building might not be right for a new one.)

- Does he come well recommended? (This is an essential question.)
- Can he take care of minor repairs himself?
- Is he experienced in collecting rents, making bank deposits, developing accurate monthly income and expense reports, readying vacant apartments, showing units to prospective tenants, answering phones, responding to tenant complaints, dealing with difficult tenants, supervising grounds maintenance and apartment repairs and maintenance, establishing good relationships with outside service people, reducing costs, and implementing energy-saving programs?

If you want a good manager who will stay with you, note how enthusiastic he is about his work and offer him a competitive salary for the area. Salaries are usually established on a per-unit basis, ranging from $5 to $10 per unit, with an apartment allowance.

Ask for a minimum of three references and check them thoroughly. It's your job—or that of the professional management company you hire—to ensure that your managers clearly understand their responsibilities.

Management Companies

The professional management company hires and fires employees, from managers to support staff; handles all rental collections; assumes responsibility for bookkeeping and reports; and oversees maintenance and repairs on the property. Charges for property-management services vary but usually range from 2 to 10 percent of monthly gross income. Check several firms in the area of your property to get an idea of the current rates.

Cutting Costs

Although increasing income from a property is a vital aspect of good management, slicing expenses is also important. In an inflationary era, holding expenses at or below existing levels is difficult, but not impossible, especially when you take over a property that hasn't been managed with a tight and careful hand.

A classic example of an expense that can run away from you if you aren't careful is the cost of utilities—water, gas, electricity, and fuel. Below are some ideas for cutting utility costs:

- Visit your local utility office and ask the energy consultants there for tips on conservation and cost-saving potentials.
- Use solar heating for swimming pools. The initial expense should be earned back quickly, for a pool is a substantial energy-eater. Also, turn pool heat down during the week, use a pool cover, and construct wind shelters for the pool.
- Wrap exterior pipes.
- Replace incandescent lights with fluorescent lights in hallways and other common areas.
- Paint hallways a light color and use lower-wattage bulbs.

- Recycle water in fountains—or get rid of the fountains.
- Adjust toilet tanks to consume less water.
- Insulate and weather-strip throughout the property.
- Review utility bills carefully to spot potential overcharges, leaks, and waste.
- Install clock timers that will automatically turn water and power on and off.
- Install a meter for each unit so the tenants pay for their own gas and power.
- Lower the temperature on water heaters and insulate them.
- Use a reflective film on windows in sunny areas.
- Insulate windows with shades or drapes.
- Use double-pane windows in cold regions.
- Use flow restrictors on faucets and shower heads.
- Landscape for energy economy, so that trees and ground cover absorb heat and use a minimum of water.

One way to evaluate your expenses is to use a bookkeeping system with progressive figures, so you can compare one month to the next and one year to the next. Some expenses, such as the cost of heating, run in high and low cycles.

If the property is big enough, a computer printout can do some checking for you. The computer can be programmed to make comparisons, which allows you to spot and evaluate increases and decreases.

Computer printouts are also helpful in presenting income figures and showing profit after expenses. Even the smallest properties need a bookkeeping system, however. For a small operation, expense records are maintained through the checkbook stubs and receipts.

The General Partner's Role in Management

Whether the property your group has purchased is in your hometown or far away, the income from it should be earning money. This is where your banker comes in.

Build up reserves for use in meeting operating expenses for the building. Rather than allow income to sit idle, arrange with the banker to get a maximum return through high-interest-bearing accounts or short-term commercial paper.

If you are a general partner, you have a fiduciary responsibility to your limited partners; that is, you must care for their investment with the utmost diligence.

As a fiduciary a general partner has specific duties in managing the group's property. For example, if the general partner hires a management company for the property, it is the general partner's job to examine all reports carefully and to make periodic visits to the site to inspect the condition of the grounds and pavement, and to be sure signs are clearly visible and refuse areas are in good shape. He should also visit the rental office and look at all vacant apartments—even if the property is out of state. It is not necessary to give advance warning every time you plan to visit. On the basis of information gleaned from reports and personal observations, the general partner can make recommendations for improvements in whatever areas seem appropriate—repairs, maintenance, tenant relations, management staff, and so forth.

An alert general partner keeps up-to-date on new materials and supplies that might benefit the property—tested products that can cut costs and improve efficiency—and on security systems. He will also stay in touch with the local attorney to check on such potential savings as property-tax reductions.

The general partner must be fastidious in maintaining entirely separate trust accounts for each property managed. It is against the law to transfer money from one account to another or in any other way to mix unrelated partnership funds.

The general partner should also be current on insurance and service contracts for the property, to be sure they are in force and offer adequate coverage. A new supplier can sometimes provide the same or better service at a lower cost.

Limited partners are entitled to quarterly reports and information on rental increases, special work on the property, changes in employees, and anything else concerning the property that might be useful to them. The material given to the limited partners might include copies of advertising for vacant units, photographs of new equipment or improvements, and articles about the property.

The general partner also is responsible for supplying limited partners with an annual tax return, an annual profit-and-loss statement, and—of course—their distribution of spendable income (the amount remaining after taking care of management fees, operating expenses, and mortgage payments). Whether or not there is spendable income, the limited partners must receive quarterly reports on how their money is being used.

I cannot overstress the importance of thorough good management. When I was a general partner for a group investment in an apartment-house complex in Texas, I found and hired an excellent property-management firm to handle all aspects of managing the complex. Then I asked the company to study the property at the time my group took possession and to report back to me recommendations concerning current policy and potential changes. Below is a synopsis of the report I received:

Management Policy

The section under "current policies" went into considerable detail about children, pets, pet deposits, security deposits, when rents were due, leasing-office hours, swimming pool hours, clubroom hours and parking.

Then the firm went into even more detail about recommended changes. It advised me to investigate prospective tenants more carefully and not to accept anybody whose "rental payment would exceed 25% of his total monthly income."

I was advised to limit pets to one per apartment, to limit pets to 20 pounds or less, to keep the leasing office open for longer hours and on Sundays and to establish adults-only hours for the swimming pool.

Re leases: "We also feel that 73 month-to-month leases are totally unacceptable. With this high percentage of month-to-month leases, the property has the potential of losing 73 residents in any one month. Although this is not probable, it certainly contributes to instability of the property. For this reason, we recommend that a staggered lease expiration schedule be established. . . ."

There were also recommendations about accepting maintenance requests on the telephone, having a designated parking area for boats and recreational vehicles, and security deposits. The management company emphatically recommended doing away with "cash for rental payment."

Physical Condition

The management company spent two and a half single-spaced pages reporting on landscaping, parking, mailboxes, fountains, elevators, etc.

Among its detailed recommendations: making tree clusters more attractive by enclosing them with railroad ties rather than boulders, moving the leasing information center, relocating the playground, making minor carpentry repairs and replacing nonworking fire extinguishers. The elevators were declared to be "in deplorable condition" and were "thoroughly cleaned, disinfected, repaired, and put on a schedule to be cleaned on a daily basis."

Marketing Analysis

After surveying eight apartment complexes in the immediate vicinity, the management company told me that my acquisition had an 83 percent occupancy rate compared to 90 percent or better at the competition. Why?

"We found on the day of our assumption of management that absolutely no marketing whatsoever was in effect for the property," said the report. "No ads were running in newspapers, magazines or on radio. No community contacts were being made. And the final blow was that the rental services which are active in the city were not bringing any prospects to the property."

Word had gotten out that my new property was the place for pets and children, but "we felt that it was not so much the . . . children and pets, but was the nature of the pets and the number of the children that created the bad reputation."

The company recommended an advertising campaign, better signs pointing the way to the leasing office, remodeling the leasing office, reminding potential residents of the property's proximity to a big expressway and reeducating the on-site staff about selling the complex's strong points.

Other recommendations included: having a party "or recreational activity for existing residents each month," offering residents a gift if they bring in a new prospect who leases an apartment, and giving bonuses to employees for each new lease or renewal they sign.

With minor exceptions I accepted the recommendations of the property-management firm, after confirming the key points during my own on-site inspection.

Tax Matters

In addition to the suggestions about policy, physical changes, and marketing direction, I asked for and received from the management firm an analysis of the property taxes, which turned up the fact that personal taxes that were due had not been paid.

Taxing authorities were advised to send all tax bills to the management company, which in turn sent copies to me. The past-due taxes, which amounted to less than $500, were paid at once. Since my sales agreement had a clause in it indemnifying the group against unpaid taxes, the seller reimbursed the group.

At the recommendation of the management firm, we hired a local accountant who was a real estate tax expert. He was able to get refunds on some previous tax payments. The amount returned more than paid his fee.

I also obtained a resident-analysis report, which gave a breakdown of the tenants by age, occupation, marital status, number of children (if any), pets, and annual income. This report provided an "average-resident profile" that was useful in evaluating the marketing plan.

The analysis showed that the largest group consisted of young people between the ages of twenty-five and thirty-four, with white-collar jobs, living alone with no children, and with incomes between $8,000 and $11,000. The next largest group was of the same age, but married or divorced, with at least one child living in the apartment. Income was in the same range. The third group, somewhat smaller but still of significant size, differed quite a bit from the first two. The average age of this group was forty-five. They lived alone, were divorced, widowed, or single, and had grown children who didn't live with them. This fact lead to speculation that there might be a good market for the apartments among older people, who could counterbalance the younger people with or without children.

Communications to Tenants

The property-management firm was also given responsibility for preparing and sending communications to the tenants. The first was a letter announcing the new ownership and the appointment of the company as leasing and management agent. The tenants were given a number to call if they had any questions and were told that rents should be paid by check or money order payable to the management firm, and that payment should be made at the resident manager's office. The final paragraph pointed out the new owners' intent to maintain the complex as "an outstanding apartment community." The next letter went to tenants who paid by cash, asking that they use a personal check, cashier's check, or money order instead.

New house rules were drawn up as a result of the studies conducted by the management firm, and each tenant received in his mailbox a complete list with explanations. The rules were also posted clearly in common areas frequented by the tenants, so that they would know what was expected of them in return for the management firm's efforts to make the complex an increasingly better and more comfortable place to live.

Necessary Forms

When it comes to the forms associated with managing a property (the lease, for example), you can either make up your own or use those of the management company. The nuts and bolts of management can be explored endlessly, but let us now look at the first steps to your own investment program.

12 Getting Rich Starting Now

*T*oday is the day to begin your real estate investment program. You've decided how much money you can invest and where your initial nest egg will come from. You've thought seriously about your goals. You have a realistic idea about how much income and profit you need and can expect from your investment. You've determined that you can have all the benefits of big property owners because you can join a group real estate investment.

Your next step is to figure out how you're going to achieve your goals. How long should you expect to wait before your income and profits fulfill your dreams? And what should you do after you reach your goals? Should you *always* invest with groups?

The advice I give to most of my clients is that they should actively invest for a given number of years, depending on their age and the amount invested when they begin. They can go into a passive investing program later on.

You can plot your own investment path by making some conservative estimates of future growth, using a pyramid chart (a chart, by the way, that is *not* related to the "pyramid club" schemes that sweep the country every twenty years or so). First I'll give you an example of how this pyramid works, starting with a foundation of the earliest group investment and building toward the top, when you might have an investment entirely on your own that provides a safe, reliable monthly income for later years.

For the example, I'll assume you begin with an investment of $20,000 in a group purchase of income-producing property. This can be residential or commercial, industrial or agricultural, but for purposes of the example I've selected commercial income-producing property.

I'll also assume that you are thirty-eight years old when you start your investment program and are looking forward to retiring at sixty. To see how your money will pyramid in a typical group investment, figured at a very conservative rate with low-risk purchases and trades, you need first to make some assumptions.

Assume that your profit from the investments is 50 percent more than you originally invested, and that this profit is taken out every three years through sale or exchange. Assume also that your tax shelter amounts to 6 percent of your investment a year and the cash flow of spendable income from the investment is also 6 percent a year. Here's how your pyramid would look:

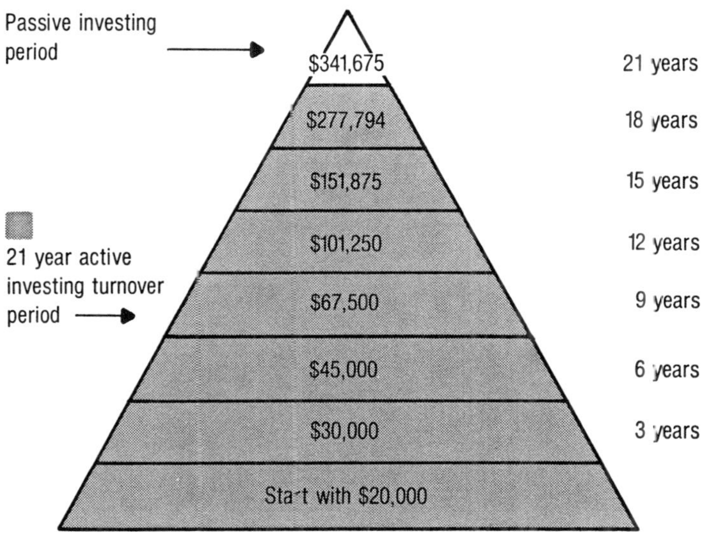

Your profit on $20,000 during the twenty-one years is not just the $321,675 more in investment value that you get after deducting the original $20,000 from $341,675. You've also had a 6-percent-a-year income from the investment, which is almost $17,000 a year by the eighteenth year, and you've had a tax deduction worth another 6 percent a year. If you reinvested the income, your pyramid would build a good deal faster.

When you reach the twenty-first year in the example, you are near retirement age and might find more peace of mind if you took back total control over your investment. Although this would involve taking on the responsibility for managing the investment, there's a way around that problem for people who prefer to avoid it.

The answer could be a net-net-net lease (also known as a triple-net lease). You buy a property and lease it to a top-rated tenant on a long-term lease. "Net-net-net" means that you lease the property with the tenant accepting responsibility for taxes, insurance, and care and maintenance of the property, plus regular cost-of-living increases in the rental payments. Anything that has to be done, short of major structural repairs, is handled—and paid for—by your tenant.

The advantages of such a lease are apparent. You have a guaranteed income from the tenant without worrying about additional expenses. You can count on that money for years and years ahead because of the long-term lease, and you know that its buying power will stay the same because you receive increases as the cost of living rises. You are the sole owner and get all the income.

You have all the advantages of a real estate investment with the protection of a reliable, steady income. You have tax-deduction benefits. Your net worth increases with the value of the property, which is an asset that can be sold if you choose to sell it. And if there's a mortgage, it diminishes and the equity builds, so that you have an increasingly valuable asset as part of your estate.

There usually comes a time when a group investor wants to stop investing with groups. At this point he might choose to set up something like the triple-net lease to provide a good income that meets goals and objectives set at the beginning of the investment program.

Realistic Figuring

You might want to sit down now with a pad of paper and figure out how your nest egg can build and how long it will take to reach your target. You have to be realistic, of course. It is doubtful that $5,000 can be increased to $1 million in ten years.

Here's how you can do your conservative estimate. (Keep in mind that it is just an estimate and that a lot of variables can affect the outcome.) We'll use the assumptions from the pyramid.

Take the dollar amount you intend to invest with the group. Divide it in two, which gives you 50 percent profit. Figure that you get that 50 percent profit every three years. Add the half to your original investment figure. Now you see what your nest egg might be in three years. Keep taking half of the total, adding it on every three years, and you will see how many years it will take to reach your goal.

To figure out how much income you might get from this amount, figure a conservative 6 percent tax shelter plus 6 percent spendable income. Multiply your investment amount by .06 to get that figure.

While you are building your fortune you will want to keep exchanging one property for a better one. This can mean taking your profit out and going to another group, or it can mean staying with the same general partner, who—with the approval of the participating limited partners—trades (exchanges) the value in one property for the value in another: equity for equity. Sometimes you'll need to put in more money, but often you will not. The only thing to watch for is that you must trade like for like. That means a general partner can't exchange his interest in one property for a limited partner interest in another. A limited partner can't exchange for a general-partner interest, either. Limited must exchange for limited, general for general: like for like.

With an exchange your profit equity is tax-deferred. You don't pay capital-gains taxes until you sell your property.

One of the key reasons for the success of group investing today is that it provides a place for the small investor to get started. If you already have $1 million, you don't have to go into a group unless you have your eye on a property that requires more than that $1 million for a down payment. Millionaires choose what they want to do, and they have no problem getting into real estate on their own.

Most people aren't millionaires, however. They are wise to go into real estate, in fact, if they want to *become* millionaires. The door to that potential is *group investment*. You pool your limited amount of money with that of others, and together you have enough to begin your ascent up the pyramid to financial freedom and security.

Reminders Before You Buy

Below is a review of the major points in this book:

1. Decide what your priorities are: spendable income, tax shelter, and/or security for the future.
2. Analyze the income and expenses of a property to determine if the result conforms to your priorities.

3. Buy where the demand for housing (or industrial or commercial property) is increasing. *Location* is almost everything.
4. Find out from your broker what other buildings in the area have been selling for, and compare with the earnings potential and price of your building.
5. Include *all* expenses, especially the unexpected ones such as uncollected rents and appliance replacements. Don't forget advertising expenses.
6. Allow for increases in utility costs and taxes. Check your projected figures with state offices and power companies.
7. Understand the nature of the numbers on the broker's listing sheet. Is rental income based on actual or projected rents?
8. Borrow the maximum. Let other people's money finance your profits.
9. Keep maintenance and modernization abreast of rent increases.
10. Watch the market and your investment. Be aware of changes.
11. Keep sight of your primary goal: making money. Don't be influenced by pride of ownership.
12. Don't sell for cash. Trade for another building with bigger profits or greater security.
13. Build a pyramid of equity. Sell/refinance/trade.

Point three deserves some comment. For years brokers have said that the three most important factors in selecting a property are location, location, and location. I'm not sure that's true anymore. There are some new elements in the game—the energy crisis, for instance. More and more people are moving back to the cities, near their work, because the suburban life-style costs too much in gasoline. That means the older neighborhoods on the edge of downtown urban areas across the nation are becoming increasingly attractive as investment sites. Close-in, marginal buildings can be rehabilitated to become office buildings, residences, commercial shopping areas, or a combination of these. Frequently, zoning permits residential *plus* business use.

Creativity with Hotels

I know a general partner who found an old hotel in a marginal part of town that was becoming more popular because it was close to where people conducted business. She fixed up the hotel by turning the lower floors into large office spaces and converting the upper floors into apartments for people who worked in or owned these businesses. Then the whole building was turned into condominiums and sold in parts—office condominiums below, residential condominiums above.

A building next door was torn down to provide parking space for residents and visitors, and that cost was built into the condo prices. Buyers flocked to the place. Business people who provided services to downtown companies loved the idea of having an apartment near the companies. It saved them time and money—*and* they didn't have to spend a fortune in gas driving to and from home. All they did was take the elevator.

The location-location-location rule would discourage this kind of enterprise, but an imaginative general partner made it a winner. Other investment groups came into the area later to build on her foundation of change.

Another story of investment creativity was a special case because the hotel was a historical landmark, one of the most unusual examples of turn-of-the-century architecture. The general partners had a great idea. There was a lot of ground around this hotel, which consisted of two buildings. They were able to take advantage of the historical-landmark law by bringing the hotel "up to code" (making it comply with the building code), preparing it for use, and taking the tax advantages given to people and/or firms that do restoration.

They divided the hotel. One building became low-cost housing for the elderly under a program of (HUD) the Department of Housing and Urban Development. The other was converted into expensive condominiums. Thus the investors were able to obtain a low-cost loan because they were doing something worthwhile for elderly, disadvantaged people, and at the same time they made a fair profit from the condos.

It pays to watch for such opportunities. Change is constant and can work for you.

A Demographic Look at the Future

Would you like to predict the future? Below are some questions, with answers backed up by extensive demographic studies done by Dr. Kingsley Davis, professor emeritus of demographics at the University of Southern California:

Q. Is it true that the United States is near zero population growth?

A. Not at all. From July 1, 1978, to July 1, 1979, population grew by almost 1.9 million people. From July 1, 1979, to July 1, 1980, another growth spurt occurred.

Q. What does this mean to the real estate investor?

A. More housing will be needed. More goods and services will be required, and facilities to house them will be needed. (That's why I make a point of saying that just about any building existing today is likely to grow in value, since construction is not keeping up with population growth and demand.)

Q. Where was the biggest population growth in the United States from 1970 to 1980?

A. The largest growth was in the mountain states, from Montana in the north to Arizona and New Mexico in the south.

Q. During that same period where was the smallest growth?

A. The mid-Atlantic and east north central states barely grew at all.

Q. What accounts for these changes?

A. People are moving into less developed areas in a continued settlement of the West. Older parts of the country have more rigid economic and social structures, and people are going to newer areas.

Q. What states are projected to have the greatest growth in the next five years?

A. Statistical analysis indicates the fastest-growing states will be Arizona, Florida, Nevada, Colorado, Alaska, Utah, Idaho, New Mexico, Wyoming, and Texas—in that order. (Setting statistics aside, I think the fastest-growing states will be those with the greatest resources in ratio to population. Those with more energy resources, for example, and lower population will probably see the greatest migration.)

Q. Where is the slowest growth over the next five years?

A. Statistics point at New York as the slowest, followed by Connecticut, Ohio, Pennsylvania, Illinois, Indiana, Iowa, South Dakota, Kansas, and Missouri. (Again, putting statistics aside, I'd look for the slowest growth in the states with the highest density of population. People don't like being crowded, so some will move into less populated areas and the number leaving will be high enough to offset any new people coming in through international migration or other movement.)

Q. What other growth patterns should be considered when choosing the site for real estate investment?

A. The highest recent population growth has been in counties with fewer than ten residents per square mile. The pattern of the 1960s, when counties with state colleges in them grew rapidly, has changed somewhat. The biggest age group is that of the now-grown "post-war babies," who are about to start families. They'll be looking for places to live and work and set up businesses.

Q. How accurate is all this information? Can it be relied on in selecting a location for a group real estate investment purchase?

A. No one can predict the future. Use this information as a guide, and bear in mind that demographic changes are less subject to radical shifts than the economy is. But a factor like the energy shortage can alter migration patterns beyond what would have been expected.

A demographer can't predict the future and neither can I. Still, I know what real estate group investing has done for me and I've seen firsthand what it has done for others. I've invested primarily in middle-income multiple dwellings. Others have done very well with commercial or industrial or other types of property.

Group investments in real estate are a way for those of us in the middle-income group to build up a fortune beyond what we could possibly gain from our jobs. We can shelter our income from overtaxation and enjoy the tax benefits once available only to the rich. (The middle-income American always bears the burden of the heaviest taxation. The tax breaks go to the wealthy.)

There's another benefit, too, one that has made group real estate investments particularly meaningful to me. I think it is special to own a piece of our country. Buying property is one of the great pluses of living in a free society like ours.

Whatever your investment capital is, whatever your investment goals are, the most important advice I can give you is to take action *now.* Today is the day for you to begin your group real estate investment adventure.

Appendix A.

State Securities Administrators

ALABAMA

Securities Commission
Director (205) 832-5733
Suite 1000, First Southern Federal Tower
100 Commerce Street
Montgomery, Alabama 36130

ALASKA

Department of Commerce and Economic Development, Division of Banking, Securities, Small Loans, and Corporations

Commissioner (907) 465-2521
Pouch D
Juneau, Alaska 99811

ARIZONA

Corporation Commission, Securities Division
Director (602) 255-4242
2222 West Encanto Boulevard
Phoenix, Arizona 85009

ARKANSAS

Securities Department
Securities Commissioner (501) 371-1011
1428 Donaghey Building
Main and Seventh Streets
Little Rock, Arkansas 72201

CALIFORNIA

Department of Corporations
Acting Commissioner (916) 445-8200
Room 205, 1025 P Street
Sacramento, California 95814

BRANCH OFFICES (Inquiries should be directed to either the San Francisco or Los Angeles branch office.)
Sixth Floor, 600 California Street (415) 557-3787
San Francisco, California 94108
600 South Commonwealth Avenue (213) 736-2741
Los Angeles, California 90005
Room 2028, 1350 Front Street (714) 236-7341
San Diego, California 92101

COLORADO

Division of Securities
Securities Commissioner (303) 839-2607
230 State Office Building
Denver, Colorado 80203

CONNECTICUT

Banking Department, Securities Division
Bank Commissioner (203) 566-5949
State Office Building
Hartford, Connecticut 06115

DELAWARE

Department of Justice, Division of Securities
Securities Commissioner (302) 571-2515
Eighth Floor, State Office Building
820 French Street
Wilmington, Delaware 19801

DISTRICT OF COLUMBIA

Public Service Commission
Chairperson (202) 727-3066
Cafritz Building
1625 I Street Northwest
Washington, D.C. 20006

FLORIDA

Department of Banking and Finance, Division of Securities
Director (904) 488-9805
Room 1402, The Capitol
Tallahassee, Florida 32304

GEORGIA

Office of Secretary of State, Securities Division
Secretary of State,
Commissioner of Securities (404) 656-2894
214 State Capitol Building
Atlanta, Georgia 30334

GUAM

Department of Revenue and Taxation, Insurance, Securities and Banking Division
Securities Administrator
P. O. Box 2796
Agana, Guam 96910

HAWAII

Department of Regulatory Agencies, Business Registration Division
Director,
Department of Regulatory Agencies (808) 548-6521
P.O. Box 40
Honolulu, Hawaii 96810

IDAHO

Department of Finance, Securities Division
Director (208) 334-3684
State Capitol Building
Boise, Idaho 83720

ILLINOIS

Office of Secretary of State, Securities Department
Secretary of State (217) 782-2256
296 Centennial Building
Springfield, Illinois 62756

INDIANA

Office of Secretary of State, Securities Division
Commissioner (317) 633-6681
102 State House
Indianapolis, Indiana 46204

IOWA

Office of Commissioner of Insurance, Securities Division
Commissioner of Insurance (515) 281-4441
Lucas State Office Building
Des Moines, Iowa 50319

KANSAS

Office of Securities Commissioner
Securities Commissioner (913) 296-3307
Suite 501
109 West Ninth Street
Topeka, Kansas 66612

KENTUCKY

Department of Banking and Securities, Division of Securities
Director (502) 564-2180
911 Leawood Drive
Frankfort, Kentucky 40601

LOUISIANA

Securities Commission
Commissioner (504) 568-5515
315 Louisiana State Office Building
325 Loyola Avenue
New Orleans, Louisiana 70112

MAINE

Department of Business Regulation, Bureau of Banking, Securities Division
Director (207) 289-2261
State Office Building
Augusta, Maine 04333

MARYLAND

Law Department, Division of Securities
Securities Commissioner (301) 383-3714
Room 602, 26 South Calvert Street
Baltimore, Maryland 21202

MASSACHUSETTS

Department of State Secretary, Securities Division
Director (617) 727-3548
1719 John W. McCormack Building
One Ashburton Place
Boston, Massachusetts 02108

MICHIGAN
Department of Commerce, Corporation and Securities Bureau, Securities Division
Director, Department of Commerce (517) 374-9417
6546 Mercantile Way
P. O. Box 30222
Lansing, Michigan 48910

MINNESOTA

Department of Commerce, Securities Division
Commissioner of Securities (612) 296-6848

Fifth Floor, Metro Square Building
Seventh and Robert Streets
St. Paul, Minnesota 55101

MISSISSIPPI

Office of Secretary of State, Securities Division
Secretary of State (601) 354-6548
106 State Executive Building
Jackson, Mississippi 39205

MISSOURI

Office of Secretary of State, Securities Division
Secretary of State (314) 751-4136
1001 Industrial Drive
Jefferson City, Missouri 65101

MONTANA

Office of Investment Commissioner
State Auditor and Investment
Commissioner (406) 449-2040
Capitol Building
Helena, Montana 59601

NEBRASKA

Department of Banking and Finance, Bureau of Securities
Director of Banking (402) 471-2171
301 Centennial Mall South
P. O. Box 95006
Lincoln, Nebraska 68509

NEVADA

Department of State, Securities Division
Secretary of State Administrator (702) 885-5203
State Capitol Building, Capitol Complex
Carson City, Nevada 89710

NEW HAMPSHIRE

Insurance Department, Securities Division
Supervisor (603) 271-2261
169 Manchester Street
Concord, New Hampshire 03301

NEW JERSEY

Department of Law and Public Safety, Division of Consumer Affairs, Bureau of Securities
Chief (201) 648-2040
Room 308, 80 Mulberry Street
Newark, New Jersey 07102

NEW MEXICO

Commerce and Industry Department, Financial Institutions Division, Securities Bureau
Chief, Securities Bureau (505) 827-5368
Lew Wallace Building
Santa Fe, New Mexico 87503

NEW YORK

Department of Law, Bureau of Securities
Attorney General (212) 488-7563
Two World Trade Center
New York, New York 10047

NORTH CAROLINA

Department of Secretary of State
Secretary of State (919) 733-3924
101 State Administration Building
Raleigh, North Carolina 27611

NORTH DAKOTA

Securities Commission
Commissioner (701) 224-2910
301 State Capitol
Bismarck, North Dakota 58505

OHIO

Department of Commerce, Division of Securities
Commissioner of Securities (614) 466-7602
Thirteenth Floor, Borden Building
180 East Broad Street
Columbus, Ohio 43215

OKLAHOMA

Securities Commission
Administrator (405) 521-2451
2915 North Lincoln Boulevard
Oklahoma City, Oklahoma 73105

OREGON

Department of Commerce, Corporation Division
Corporation Commissioner (503) 378-4387
Commerce Building
158 12th Street N.E.
Salem, Oregon 97310

PENNSYLVANIA

Securities Commission
Chairman (717) 787-6828
471 Education Building
Harrisburg, Pennsylvania 17109
BRANCH OFFICES
1109 Philadelphia State Office Building (215) 238-3680
Broad and Spring Garden Streets
Philadelphia, Pennsylvania 19130
806 State Office Building (412) 565-5083
Pittsburgh, Pennsylvania 15222

PUERTO RICO

Department of the Treasury, Bureau of Securities
Administrator (809) 725-4075
Room 708, Seventh Floor
Intendente Alejandro Ramirez Building
P. O. Box 4515
San Juan, Puerto Rico 00905

RHODE ISLAND

Department of Business Regulation, Banking Division, Securities Section
Chief Securities Examiner (401) 277-2405
100 North Main Street
Providence, Rhode Island 02903

SOUTH CAROLINA

Department of State, Securities Division
Secretary of State and
Securities Commissioner (803) 758-2833
816 Keenan Building
Columbia, South Carolina 29201

SOUTH DAKOTA

Department of Commerce and Consumer Affairs, Division of Securities
Director (605) 773-3241
State Capitol Building
Pierre, South Dakota 57501

TENNESSEE

Department of Insurance, Division of Loans and Securities
Commissioner of Insurance (615) 741-2947
114 State Office Building
Nashville, Tennessee 37219

TEXAS

State Securities Board
Securities Commissioner (512) 474-2233
1800 San Jacinto Street
P. O. Box 13167, Capitol Station
Austin, Texas 78711

UTAH

Department of Business Regulation, Securities Commission
Director of Securities (801) 533-4239
330 East Fourth South Street
Salt Lake City, Utah 84111

VERMONT

Department of Banking and Insurance, Securities Division
Commissioner of Banking
and Insurance (802) 828-3301
State Office Building
Montpelier, Vermont 05602

VIRGINIA

State Corporation Commission, Division of Securities and Retail Franchising
Director (804) 786-7751
Shockoe Center Building
11 South 12th Street
Richmond, Virginia 23219

WASHINGTON

Department of Licensing, Business and Professions Administration, Securities Section
Director, Department of Licensing (206) 753-6928
P. O. Box 648
Olympia, Washington 98504

WEST VIRGINIA

State Auditor's Office, Securities Division
State Auditor,
Commissioner of Securities (304) 348-2257
W205 State Capitol Building
Charleston, West Virginia 25305

WISCONSIN

Office of Commissioner of Securities
Commissioner (608) 266-3431
111 West Wilson Street
P. O. Box 1768
Madison, Wisconsin 53701

WYOMING

Office of Secretary of State
Secretary of State and
Securities Administrator (307) 777-7378
State Capitol Building
Cheyenne, Wyoming 82002

Appendix B: Glossary

Acceleration Clause: The clause in the mortgage that declares the entire outstanding mortgage indebtedness due upon a default of the mortgagee in making payment of any installment at the time required in the mortgage terms.

Acquisition Expenses: Costs involved in acquiring property, such as surveys, travel expenses, escrow charges, and legal expenses.

Acquisition Fee: Money paid to syndicator for arranging the acquisition of a property.

Advances: Money advanced by the lender to pay real estate taxes or other costs to protect the lender's interest.

Alienation Clauses: A specific type of acceleration clause where total loan balance becomes due upon the sale or transfer of title. Also known as Due-on-Sale Clause.

Amenities: One or more pleasant or desirable qualities which increase the value of real estate to the owner (seller or purchaser).

Amortization: The repayment of debt in period installments. "Full amortization" means the principal and interest payments are spread across the entire length of the loan, and the initial loan amount and the required interest are fully paid by these periodic payments.

Annual Percentage Rate: Standardized disclosure of the total cost of a loan to the borrower, demanded by Truth-in-Lending laws.

Annuity: A series of equal payments made over a period of time.

Antideficiency Legislation: Statutes that prohibit a lender from obtaining a judgment for money against a defaulting borrower under a deed of trust.

Appraisal: A written estimate or opinion of value prepared by an individual who is qualified to give such an opinion.

Appreciation Build-up: An increase in value due to inflation and supply and demand factors. Always a speculative estimate.

Assessments: *See* Property Assessments.

Assignment of Interest: An instrument that transfers the beneficial interest from one party to another.

Assignment of Mortgage: The lender (mortgagee) who holds the mortgage may sell it intact to another investor.

Assignment of Rents: The transfer of title to the rents from an income property where the lease agreements remain undisturbed by the recipient and owner of the contracted rents changes. The assignment of rents clause in a mortgage refers to the automatic transfer of ownership of the rent receipts from the mortgagor to the mortgagee upon proven mortgage default.

Assumption of Deed of Trust or Mortgage: Assumption, upon taking title to a property, of the responsibility and liability for the payment of the existing deed of trust or mortgage.

Assumption Fee: A lender's charge for changing and processing records for a new owner who is assuming an existing loan.

Average Annual Return on Equity: Other labels for the same investment measure are "Cash Return on

Equity" and "Cash on Cash Return." The annual projected net cash flow is divided by the cash equity in the project.

Balloon Payment: When a mortgage loan is not fully amortized over the term of the loan, a sizable payment on the principal is due at the loan maturity.

Bank: A commercial or mutual savings institution.

Basis: Property owner's "book value" for income tax purposes. (Original cost plus capital improvements, less depreciation.)

Beneficiary: A lender under a note secured by a deed of trust.

Blanket Deed of Trust or Mortgage: A single trust deed or mortgage which covers more than one parcel of real estate.

Blind Pool: Investors' money is pooled to acquire unknown properties.

Blue Sky: Legal slang for laws and regulations concerning the protection of the public against the imposition of insubstantial schemes and the securities based on them.

Boot: The taxable cash or other "unlike" property received in an exchange of property.

Break-even Point: Debt service and operating expenses divided by gross income.

Broker: In relation to real estate, any person acting for others in return for compensation.

Broker's Loan Statement: A statement signed and received by the borrower at the time of a loan transaction, indicating the costs and deductions, including commissions, of a loan negotiated by a real estate licensee.

Capital Gain: Unrealized receivable, or substantially appreciated items.

Capital Investment or Contribution: Either the initial amount invested by a particular investor at the time of the partnership's organization, or the investor's *continuing* or *total* investment.

Capitalization: The total sum of money to be contributed by the investors, including both down payment and additional commitment as called for in the partnership agreement and/or offering circular.

Cash Flow: Actual surplus or spendable dollars remaining in an investment property after all expenses have been met.

Closed End: An offering or fund which, after the sale of a maximum number of units, is "closed," with no additional units to be offered to issue without further amendment of the agreement of partnership. An Open End offering would indicate that further securities can be issued without amending or changing the partnership agreement.

Closing Costs: Costs paid by buyers, sellers, and borrowers on the sale of a property.

Collateral: Security given for fulfillment of a debt or obligation.

Commercial Bank: General purpose lenders chartered by state or federal governments.

Commission on Interests: A commission paid for the sale of Syndicate Interests to investors.

Commission on Property: A commission by the seller to the broker on the sale of the real property.

Common Area: Universally owned property as stated in agreement with mutual buyers.

Conditional Sale Contract: A contract of sale giving possession to the buyer, with legal title remaining with the seller until the conditions of the contract have been fulfilled.

Condominium Unit: The airspace bounded by the four walls, ceiling, and floor, which may be owned in fee simple and is usually described on a recorded plat for a condominium-type building. The individual unit can be financed separately by its owner.

Construction Loan: A loan which finances construction of improvements to land, such as buildings.

Contingency: The state of something likely, but not certain, to happen.

Conventional Mortgage Loan: A loan which is not guaranteed by the Veterans Administration or insured by FHA's Mutual Mortgage Insurance Corporation. It may be insured by a private mortgage insurance company.

Co-op Sale: A sale involving more than one broker, with consequent sharing of commission.

Cooperative Apartment Ownership: The cooperative unit owner holds a portion of the proprietary lease of the total cooperative building, buys the shares of beneficial interest associated with the value of his cooperative unit, and assumes the portion of the master mortgage assigned to his cooperative unit.

Correspondent: *See* Mortgage Loan Correspondent.

Co-signer: A person other than the borrower who signs a note to provide additional security. The co-signer is also liable for the repayment of the loan. Also known as co-maker.

Cost: The amount of dollars expended to develop or acquire a property.

Debenture: Bonds issued without security and backed only by the credit standing and earning capacity of the issuer.

Debt Service: Required periodic payments established by the mortgage note.

Debt Service Coverage: The ratio of net income before debt service and taxes, divided by debt service.

Deed of Reconveyance: Transference of legal title from lender to borrower upon the repayment of a promissory note secured by a deed of trust.

Deed of Trust: A three-party real estate financing contract where title to real estate is transferred to third party as security for a real estate loan.

Default: Failure to make the payments on a real estate loan.

Demographics: Relating to the dynamic balance of population.

Depreciation: Systematic allocation of the cost of some asset over the accounting periods making up its useful life.

Developer: Usually the single individual who has the experience and background in real estate project development.

Discount: An amount deducted from a loan by the lender before the borrower is given the money. Also referred to as points, since the amount is determined by percentage.

Double-Declining Depreciation: The depreciation allowance based upon a rate which is double the straight-line depreciation rate.

Due-on-Sale Clause: *See* Alienation Clause.

Easement: A right of way which one individual has in property of another.

Economic Life: Profit earning period of land improvements.

Economic Obsolescence: *See* Environmental Obsolescence.

Effective Age: The age assigned to the improvements by the appraiser, not necessarily the chronological age.

Effective Gross Income: Estimated potential gross revenue for a real estate investment, less a reasonable vacancy and bad debt allowance.

Encroachment: Any physical object which extends into the property of another.

Encumbrance: Any claim which affects or limits the fee-simple title to real property.

Equity Build-up: The equity acquired in a property through the repayment of the mortgage principal as a part of the debt service payments.

Equity of Redemption: The common-law right of paying the outstanding mortgage indebtedness, as well as court costs and accumulated interest, within a stated time period after the mortgage default and/or the foreclosure sale.

Excess Depreciation: The excess of depreciation taken on an accelerated basis over a straight-line basis.

Exchange: Under a current tax law two or more properties of like kind can be exchanged or traded rather than sold and tax will be deferred until actual sale.

Exculpatory Clause: A clause in a mortgage or lease that the borrower or lessee has no personal liability and that the lender or lessor will look only to the property for repayment.

Expense Ratio: The ratio between total expenses, exclusive of mortgage debt, to total gross income.

Favorable Leverage: The use of someone else's money for a price or interest rate which is less than the rate of return earned with the use of the money.

Feasibility Study: The economic study of a proposed real estate project in order to estimate the potential or expected investment yield.

Fee Simple Determinable: The fee simple automatically terminated on the happening of a stated event. The estate goes back to the grantor.

Fiduciary: A person in a position of trust, such as between a principal and his agent.

First Deed of Trust of Mortgage: The first recorded loan, which takes precedence over junior loans or second loans.

First Refusal: Provision in a partnership agreement for partners to have the first opportunity to purchase the interest of the other partners before such interest is offered to any outside party.

Foreclosure: The selling of properties pledged as security by a defaulting borrower in order to pay the debt.

Fractionalization: In selling his interest an investor may further divide his unit and sell less than a single unit. Many partnerships contain clauses prohibiting fractionalization.

Front End Load: Tax benefits taken in first year or cash compensation taken by syndicator for setting up syndicate.

Functional Obsolescence: This type of depreciation represents loss of property value from some defective factor within the property itself, which leads to less livability and occupant satisfaction. Examples are obsolete wiring of a home or poor room layout.

Gap Loan: The loan which finances the real estate between the completion of construction and the acquisition of the permanent loan commitment.

General Partners: In a Limited Partnership, the person (or persons) who bears all personal liability in connection with the partnership.

Gross Income: Total income of a property prior to expenses and debt service.

Gross Income Multiplier: The factor calculated by dividing sales price by annual gross income.

Gross Rent Multiplier: The factor calculated by dividing price by monthly rental income.

Ground Lease: Land rented on a long-term basis.

Highest and Best Use: The use of a property which gives the land its highest value. The use of a property which affords the maximum net present value of the expected net cash flows.

Hobbies and Hobby Treatment: Those transactions which the IRS determines were not entered into for the purpose of making a profit are called "hobbies" and are not tax deductible.

Hog Line: The point at which the compensation paid to a syndicator becomes unreasonable.

Homeowners Association: The organization of condominium or cooperative unit owners from the building or project which (1) decides upon the repairs and maintenance service needed, (2) contracts for landscape service and other services used for building upkeep, and (3) manages the building or project after the developer turns the management over to the association when the building units are sold.

Hypothecate: To use something for security in a loan yet not give up possession, such as when real estate is used as security or collateral in a trust deed.

Impound Account: Funds sometimes collected by lender with mortgage payment and placed in separate account in order to pay for taxes and insurance.

Income Approach to Appraising: If a property generates income, the income approach to appraising is the method of estimating the present worth of the future benefits of the property.

Indemnify: To give security against the consequences of illegal acts.

Installment Sale: According to the IRS, an installment sale is one in which the total purchase price is received by the seller over a number of years. (For maximum amounts of first and subsequent payments, see latest IRS ruling.)

Institution: A formal establishment dealing with money and loans, such as banks, insurance companies, and pension plans, as opposed to private parties.

Interim Financing: A construction loan usually due at the completion of the project. Often paid off by taking out a more conventional mortgage loan.

Intermediate Loan: A short-term loan taken out under unfavorable loan conditions but to be replaced later by a favorable long-term loan.

Joint Venture: A combination of partners for a real estate venture which provides access to short-term and long-term mortgage funds, equity, and development expertise.

Junior Loan: Those loans which are secondary to "senior encumbrances."

Kiting: When two sale contracts are made at same time, one at the true purchase price and the other at a higher price, to obtain a larger loan from the lender.

Land Contract: The real estate contract which is utilized by a seller of property when he or she may wish to finance the sale and, at the same time, retain title until an adequate amount of the purchase price has been paid by the buyer.

Land Loan: A loan with which land is purchased.

Late Charge: Charge for late payment of a regular loan installment.

Lease: A written or oral agreement setting forth the conditions concerning occupancy of property. In many jurisdictions any lease for more than one year must be in writing. A Master Lease is one in which the tenant may sublease the property. A Straight Lease is one in which the lessee has no rights to sublease. A Gross Lease is one in which the lessor pays all the expenses. A Net Lease is a lease in which the tenant pays all the expenses.

Leaseback: Where the seller leases back the property after sale. Provides financing and tax advantages.

Leasehold Estate: The rights the lessee has in the property owned by the lessor.

Letter of Intent: A nonobligatory expression of intent to invest.

Leverage: Where the actual value of the property is greater than the original cash investment for it. The difference is made up of loans.

Lien: A specific kind of encumbrance. A lien is a claim which one person has upon the property of another as security for a debt or outstanding obligation, such as taxes or a mortgage.

Limited Partnerships: A type of partnership in which the general partners with full financial liability manage the partnership while the limited partners with limited liability contribute the money to the investment venture.

Liquidity: The ease with which an investment can be converted to cash.

Loan Closing: Occurs when all conditions of the loan are approved, monies are transferred to the principals, title changes hands to the new owner, and all documents are recorded in the appropriate local government office.

Loan Commitment: An agreement by a lender to make loans at a certain rate, providing that specific conditions are met.

Loan Fee: A charge for processing loan by lender. Part of the closing costs.

Loan Package: All the forms and documents necessary for the lender to make a decision regarding making a loan.

Loan-to-Value Ratio: Under certain government regulations, institutional lenders may make loans only up to a percentage of the total purchase price.

Lock-in Clause: A clause in a loan that does not allow the loan to be paid off until after a specified period of time.

Major Lease: An income property which is negotiated by a high-credit-rated tenant, who is usually a national or regional chain with a well-established financial and merchandising reputation.

Management Fee: Paid to oversee the management of a syndicated group or property. May be determined by a percentage of income.

Market Value: The highest price estimated in terms of money which a property will bring if exposed for sale in the open market, with a reasonable time allowed to find a purchaser buying with full knowledge of all the purposes to which the property is capable of being used, when the buyer and seller are under no unusual pressure.

Master Lease: *See* Lease.

Maturity: Reached when a negotiable instrument such as a real estate note becomes due. The maturity of an investment would be the projected resale date.

Mobile Home: A manufactured house which is equipped with wheels for transport of the home by highway.

Mortgage: A lien against the borrower's real property in return for funds from the lender.

Mortgage Amortization: The repayment of the principal of the loan. There may be a schedule of amortization for a period equal to the life of the loan.

Mortgage Company: A financial institution that works as an intermediary who originates loans and usually sells the entire inventory to local or distant investors. Very little money is invested in mortgages and then it is usually on a short-term basis.

Mortgage Loan: A loan in which real estate is pledged as collateral.

Mortgage Loan Correspondent: A mortgage banker who services loans as an agent for the owner of the mortgage.

Mortgage Note: The contract in which the mortgagor promises to repay the loan principal plus interest to the mortgagee. The terms of repayment are established in the mortgage note.

Mortgage Package: All the terms connected with a mortgage, including the nominal or stated interest rate, the term of the loan, the loan-to-value ratio, the mortgage insurance, the fees and charges for loan origination, and the discount points.

Net Lease: *See* Lease.

Net Operating Income: Vacancy allowances, estimated bad debt loss, and operating expenses are subtracted from gross potential income. Net operating income is the equivalent to cash flow before depreciation, taxes, and debt service requirements.

Open End: *See* Closed End.

Option: A contract held by the optionee which gives the right to buy or lease from the landowner (the optioner) according to the terms stated in the contract.

Optioner: The person gaining the right to buy or lease from the landowner on the basis of the option contract.

Originator Fee: The fee paid by the prospective borrower to the lender or lender correspondent for setting up the mortgage.

Permanent Loan: A long-term mortgage loan which may fund the previous short-term loans on the real estate project. This type of loan can run for twenty to thirty years.

Personal Property: Assets which are not real properties, but are mobile and sometimes intangible.

Physical Deterioration: The decline in property value from the physical wear and tear on the building. Physical deterioration, which is a form of depreciation, may be curable.

Points: A point is 1 percent of the amount of a mortgage loan. Points are deducted in advance from the full amount of the loan and are a one-time cost paid by the borrower in order to obtain the loan. Interest will be charged on the full amount of the loan.

Power of Eminent Domain: The power of acquisition of property title from private landowners for public good. Usually the sale of the necessary property is involuntary, and the local authority condemns the property for the public acquisition.

Prepayment Penalty: The lender exacts a penalty for the prepayment of the mortgage. Prepayment means payment of the required debt service before the due date of the mortgage loan agreement.

Price: The amount of dollars paid for a property, which may or may not be indicative of the market value.

Primary Mortgage Market: The mortgage market in which the mortgage terms are negotiated between the borrower and the lender, or the lender correspondent, and the mortgage loan is closed.

Profit: The amount usually subject to federal income taxes. Taxable income. Net operating income less mortgage interest and depreciation.

Property Assessment: Taxes by government agencies or districts as charges for improvements.

Proprietorship: The ownership of property by a single person.

Real Estate: The land and everything attached, above and below the earth's surface.

Real Estate Appraisal: The report of estimated value for a real property as of a given date.

Real Estate Investment: The purchase of real property with the intent to receive a return or yield from the investment as well as the return of the purchase price.

Real Estate Syndicate: A combination of property owners who individually own syndicate shares and whose monies are invested by the syndicate manager in real estate projects which promise reasonably good yields to each of the syndicate members.

Real Property: The interest benefits and rights inherent in the ownership of the real estate. Real property is the bundle of rights with which real estate is owned.

Recapture: Being able to use all of a property's potential depreciation for income tax purposes.

Recapture Clause: A clause in a lease that allows a tenant to deduct certain expenses from rent.

Recurring Closing Costs: *See* Nonrecurring Closing Costs.

Refinance: To replace existing financing.

Registration: Certain investments must be registered if they are exchanged across state borders.

Reinstatement: When a borrower reinstates a loan that had entered default proceedings.

Reinvestment Clause: A clause in a partnership agreement which states that income generated may be reinvested.

Replacement Cost: The cost of replacing the property being appraised with one having equivalent utility and amenities.

Reproduction Cost: The amount of expenditure required for the faithful reconstruction of the improvements precisely like the original improvements.

Reserve: Money placed in reserve to be used for a specific purpose, such as to replace items which wear out.

Resident Manager: A person living on the premises to care for the project.

Return on Investment: The ratio consisting of profit or net operating income divided by the initial investment.

Sale Leaseback: An arrangement whereby the proposed tenant builds his own building or has the prospective owner build the structure to the tenant's specifications. The tenant sells the building to the investor immediately upon completion and leases it back on a long-term basis.

Savings and Loan Associations: State or federally regulated institutions primarily designed to give real estate loans from depositors' funds.

Secondary Financing: A loan secured by a junior trust deed or mortgage.

Secondary Mortgage Market: The purchase and selling of existing trust deeds and mortgages.

Sheltered Income: *See* Tax Shelter Investment

Standing Mortgage: A mortgage where the payments are of interest only and there is no reduction of principal.

Straight-line Depreciation: An equal amount of depreciation is taken each year of the economic life of the depreciable asset. The rate is determined by dividing the number of years of the economic life into the number one.

Subordinated Interest: An interest which is junior to the interests of the other investors. The other investors will receive a return before the subordinated interest can participate in the distribution of cash and assets.

Syndicate: The form of organization for joint investment in real estate by a number of syndicate investors, in which a syndicate manager selects the investment properties, sells the syndicate shares, and buys and operates the properties for the benefit of the syndicate members, for a management fee.

Syndicator: A person or entity involved in the formation or management of a syndicate.

Taxable Income: Income considered for tax purposes which has had all available deductions.

Tax Deference: Income received on which no tax is paid until years later. It is thought that when the tax is paid it will be at a lower rate. Retirement funds are a form of tax deference.

Tax-Deferred Installment Sale: Under certain conditions specified in IRS ruling 1031, equities of properties may be traded and all taxes deferred until resale of the property.

Tax Loss: Loss shown on a tax return that does not necessarily mean a cash loss occurred. Tax loss can be caused by depreciation offsetting actual cash profit.

Tax Shelter Investment: A real estate investment which shows a negative tax position whose loss can be transferred to other tax-bearing investments or earnings. A real estate investment where the reduced tax burden from the tax deduction of depreciation equals the loan amortization.

Tiered Financing: When several levels of financing are used, such as a loan on the property and a first and second mortgage on the improvements.

Tight Money: When demand for loans exceeds availability, interest rates increase and the qualifications of the borrowers become more difficult to meet.

Title: Legal record of ownership specifying kind of ownership (sole and separate, joint tenancy, tenants in common, corporate, etc.).

Title Insurance: A title company will give insurance against title defects.

Triple A Tenant: Rating from a credit rating bureau indicating an excellent credit rate.

Trust Deed: A security agreement for financing with real estate as collateral and a trustee to hold the property title until the mortgage terms are completed. The other term for the security agreement is "deed of trust."

Trustee Sale: Foreclosure sale due to default.

Trustor: Borrower in a trust deed loan who deeds property to the trustee.

Unfavorable Leverage: The use of someone else's money at an interest rate which is more than the rate of return earned with the use of that money.

Unit: The number of rental spaces in a building. Also refers to the smallest equal share of an investment. Usually the minimum purchase available.

Unsecured Loan: A loan given that is not secured by note, trust deed, or mortgage.

Unspecified Fund: See Blind Pool.

Usury: Refers to a loan at a rate of interest above the maximum available rate. Governed by state statutes.

Vacancy Factors: An actual or estimated percentage of vacant units.

Variable Interest Rate: A loan where the interest rate is allowed to change to better reflect the current market. Eases money in a tight market situation.

Variable Rate Mortgage: A mortgage whose interest varies every established period according to the movement of a money- and capital-market index.

Wraparound Loan: (Also known as All-Inclusive Deed of Trust.) An arrangement in which the seller provides a mortgage loan to the buyer for the full sale value of the property, less cash down. Any existing mortgage will be included in this total mortgage and the seller will retain the difference between interest charged on the existing loan and the interest that will be charged the new buyer.

Write-Off: Deductions from income used to reduce income taxes.

Yield: Usually the annual cash flow return of an investment, but sometimes computed in after-tax terms which can be greater due to deductible tax losses.

Appendix C.

When recorded return to:
Urbane Real Estate
2345 Elm Terrace
Los Angeles, California 90049

CERTIFICATE OF LIMITED PARTNERSHIP OF PLACE PORTSMOUTHE DEVELOPMENT, LTD., A LIMITED PARTNERSHIP

We, the undersigned, being desirous of forming a Limited Partnership, pursuant to the Uniform Limited Partnership Act, do hereby certify:

1. The name of the firm under which this Partnership is to be conducted is PORTSMOUTHE DEVELOPMENT LTD., A LIMITED PARTNERSHIP.

2. The character of the business intended to be transacted by the Partnership is the acquisition, ownership, and operation of income-producing real property.

3. The location of the principal place of business is to be at 2345 Elm Terrace, Los Angeles, California 90049.

4. The name and residence of the General Partners interested in the Partnership are set forth on the attached Exhibit "A."

5. The name and place of residence of each Limited Partner is set forth on the attached Exhibit "A."

6. The term of the Partnership is to continue until February 1, 2020, unless earlier terminated under the terms of the Limited Partnership Agreement.

7. The amount of cash contributed by each of the Limited Partners is set forth on the attached Exhibit "A."

8. There are no additional contributions agreed to be made by any of the Limited Partners.

9. The contribution of each Limited Partner is to be made upon the formation of the Partnership.

10. The share of the profits to be received by each Limited Partner is shown on the attached Exhibit "A".

11. A Limited Partner has a right to substitute an assignee as a substituted Limited Partner in his place and stead on condition that such substitution is approved by the General Partners and the proposed substituted Limited Partner agrees to the terms of the Limited Partnership Agreement.

12. The General Partners have a right to substitute additional Limited Partners.

13. There is no right of priority as among the Limited Partners.

14. The remaining General Partner or Partners have a right to continue the business upon the death, retirement, or insanity of a General Partner or a Partner.

15. The Limited Partners have no right to demand or receive property other than cash in return for any capital contribution.

16. The Limited Partners have no right to participate in management decisions affecting business of the Partnership.

IN WITNESS THEREOF, the undersigned have executed this Certificate on ——, 1979.

GENERAL PARTNERS:

* * *

LIMITED PARTNERSHIP AGREEMENT OF PORTSMOUTHE DEVELOPMENT, LTD., A LIMITED PARTNERSHIP

THIS LIMITED PARTNERSHIP AGREEMENT made and entered into this ____ day of ______ 1979, by and between the parties hereto, confirms that such parties have agreed among themselves to form a Limited Partnership for the purposes and upon the terms, covenants, and conditions hereinafter set forth. For purposes of this Agreement the following definitions shall be applicable unless otherwise indicated:

The term "partnership property" shall mean the real and personal property to be acquired from time to time by the Partnership.

The terms "profit" and "loss" mean for any given period the profit and loss of the Partnership as reported upon by the Certified Public Accountant regularly employed by the Partnership and determined in accordance with the Partnership's usual accounting practices (which shall be on the cash basis used for federal income tax purposes) and applied on a consistent basis.

1. THE PARTNERSHIP

The partners do hereby join themselves as Limited Partners in accordance with the provisions of the Uniform Limited Partnership Act.

2. NAME

The name of this Partnership is PORTSMOUTHE DEVELOPMENT LTD., A LIMITED PARTNERSHIP, or such other name as the partners may subsequently determine by unanimous consent.

3. PRINCIPAL PLACE OF BUSINESS

The principal place of business is hereby designated as 2345 Elm Terrace, Los Angeles, California 90049, or at such other location as the Managing General Partners shall designate.

4. PARTNERSHIP PURPOSE

Without limiting any of the activities of the Partnership, the general purpose for which the partnership is formed is the acquisition, ownership, development, operation, and sale of certain real property located in the State of Texas.

5. CERTIFICATE OF LIMITED PARTNERSHIP

The partners may, concurrently with the execution of this Agreement, sign and acknowledge a Certificate of Limited Partnership pursuant to the provisions of the Uniform Limited Partnership Act. In the alternative, such Certificate may be signed and acknowledged by SAM BARKER and/or JOHN JONES in accordance with Paragraph 22 of this Agreement. The General Partners shall thereafter cause said Certificate to be filed for record in the office of the Recorder of the county in which the principal place of business of the Partnership is situated. The recorded Certificate of Limited Partnership, or a copy thereof certified by the Recorder for the above mentioned county, shall also be filed for record in the office of the Recorder of each other county in which real property to which it holds title is situated. The Certificate shall be amended or cancelled as required by the above mentioned Uniform Limited Partnership Act. Without limiting any provisions of this Agreement, any writing to amend the Certificate of Partnership to add or substitute a Limited Partner may be executed by the individual or individuals mentioned above in the same manner as the original Certificate.

6. TERM

The partnership shall commence as of the date upon which this Limited Partnership Agreement is fully executed and shall continue for a period ending on the earliest of the following dates:

A. February 1, 2020;

B. The date on which all the property owned by the Partnership is sold or otherwise disposed of;

C. The date on which the partnership is dissolved pursuant to any provisions of this Agreement; or

D. The date on which the Partnership is dissolved by operation of law or judicial decree.

7. DESIGNATION OF PARTNERS

The partners, General and Limited to this Partnership, are designated and their respective addresses are shown on the attached Exhibit "A", incorporated herein by reference as if set forth in full.

8. CAPITAL CONTRIBUTIONS

The capital contributions of each of the partners to the Partnership is set forth on the attached Exhibit "A", incorporated herein by reference as if set forth in full.

9. WITHDRAWAL OF CAPITAL

Except as provided herein, no capital of the Partnership may be withdrawn by any partner without the express written consent of all of the partners.

10. INTEREST ON CAPITAL

No partner shall be entitled to interest on his contributions to the capital of this Partnership.

11. LOANS TO PARTNERSHIP

A partner or partners may lend or advance money to or for the benefit of the Partnership with the approval of all of the partners, and such loan shall be segregated in a loans payable account. Interest shall be payable on all such loans at ten percent (10%) per annum.

12. PARTICIPATION IN PROFITS AND LOSSES

The profits and losses of the Partnership, which are to be determined by a Certified Public Accountant engaged by the Partnership in accordance with generally accepted accounting practices, shall be allocated and borne in accordance with those percentages set forth in the attached Exhibit "A".

13. DISTRIBUTIONS

All distributions are to be made in accordance with the exercise of discretion by the Managing General Partners in accordance with the management provisions of this Agreement. As to all distributions from the Partnership from operating revenue, the following priority of distribution shall prevail:

A. To current liabilities of the Partnership, including any loans made to the Partnership by any Partner;

B. To establish a reasonable reserve for any existing long-term obligations of the Partnership;

C. To the Partners in accordance with their rights to distribution as reflected in Exhibit "A".

As to all other distributions from the Partnership (from whatever source and for whatever reason such distribution may be made, including refinance or sale), the following priority of distribution shall prevail:

A. To current liabilities of the Partnership, including any loans made to the Partnership by any Partner;

B. To establish a reasonable reserve for any existing long-term obligations of the Partnership;

C. To all of the Partners to be distributed among them to the extent required to effect full, complete, and total return of their respective cash capital contributions;

D. Thereafter, to all of the Partners in accordance with their rights to participate in profits and losses as shown in Exhibit "A."

14. MANAGEMENT

JOHN JONES and SAM BARKER are hereby designated as joint Managing General Partners of the Partnership. The Managing General Partners shall have charge of the affairs of the Partnership and shall operate its business for the benefit of all of the partners. The Managing General Partners shall have authority to act on behalf of the Partnership as to its day-to-day operation and shall have the authority, subject to such limitations as may be imposed by reason of their fiduciary duty, to expend Partnership funds in the furtherance of the business of the Partnership, sell or encumber Partnership assets, and to take such acts as may be reasonably required to effect the purpose of the Partnership. In this connection the Managing General Partners may employ such agents, employees, contractors, attorneys, and accountants as they may deem reasonably required to carry out the business of the Partnership. In the exercise of their management functions as described in this provision and as provided by law, the Managing General Partners shall concur with respect to the conduct of the Partnership business. The Limited Partners, and each of them, shall take no part in the management and conduct of the Partnership business and shall have no right or authority to act on behalf of the Partnership or purport to bind the Partnership. The Managing General Partners may, in the exercise of their discretion, elect to add additional Limited Partners to the Partnership. The grant of management authority to the Managing General Partners shall not be construed as an undertaking by any of the General Partners to provide full-time services for the benefit of the Partnership. No Partner shall be required to expend any time or effort for the benefit of the Partnership other than that time or effort required to comply with the terms of this Agreement and it is expressly understood that each of the Partners is at liberty to conduct his or her own business and to participate in other investments and to actively engage in other ventures.

15. SALARIES

No Partner shall receive any salary, commission, or fee for their management services. All reasonable expenses of Partnership operations and the expenses of maintenance and operation of the Partnership's real and personal property shall be paid by the Partnership.

16. BANK ACCOUNT

Partnership funds shall be deposited in the name of the Partnership in one or more banks, savings and loan associations, or other financial institutions to be designated by the Managing General Partners and shall be withdrawn upon the signature of any one of the Managing General Partners.

17. BOOKS OF ACCOUNT

The Partnership shall maintain at the office of the Partnership or of its accountant, books, records, and accounts which fairly present the operation of the Partnership on a cash basis, as such term is commonly understood in the accounting profession. The books shall be available for inspection by any partner, general or limited, or the representative of any partner at all reasonable times. The Managing General Partners shall have the right, in their absolute discretion, to elect which method shall be used to calculate depreciation of any depreciable Partnership assets.

18. TRANSFER OF INTEREST OF GENERAL PARTNERS

No interest of the General Partners shall be assignable or transferable except with the express written consent of all of the Partners; provided, however, that should any such interest be transferred by operation of law, or by reason of death or incapacity of such General Partner, the remaining Partners may, by majority determination, elect to approve such transfer upon the assumption by the proposed transferee of all of the obligations and duties of the transferor, or in the alternative, may elect to approve such transfer and treat such transferee as a Limited Partner and thereafter such interest so transferred shall be construed in all respects as a Limited Partner's interest, subject to the provisions of Paragraph 19 below. Excepting as to rights relating to management, any such transfer so approved, or assignment made with the consent of the partners, shall not affect the rights of the assignee or transferee to participate in profits or losses, or to exercise any other rights under the terms of this Agreement. To the extent permitted by law, any General Partner, other than the Managing General Partners, may elect to modify the character of his or her interest from that of a General Partner to that of a Limited Partner subject to the express written approval of the remaining General Partners. Such modification shall not affect such partner's rights to participate in profits and losses as defined in Exhibit "A".

19. TRANSFER OF LIMITED PARTNERS' INTEREST

The interest of the Limited Partner may be sold, assigned, or transferred, provided, however, that such assignee or transferee shall not become a "substituted Limited Partner" unless and until such assignee or transferee shall have executed a written agreement agreeing to comply with the terms and conditions of this Agreement to be performed by said Limited Partner and such substitution has been approved by the Managing General Partners.

20. DISSOLUTION OF THE PARTNERSHIP

The partnership shall dissolve and terminate upon the occurrence of any one of the following events:

A. Election by a surviving General Partner not to continue the business pursuant to the terms of this Agreement;

B. Any act of insolvency on the part of, or the dissolution or retirement of, both the General Partners; or

C. Expiration of the term of the Partnership.

21. WINDING UP OF THE PARTNERSHIP

Upon dissolution of the Partnership, the General Partners shall wind up the Partnership's affairs by liquidating its assets and making distribution in accordance with Paragraph 13 of this Agreement.

22. EXECUTION OF DOCUMENTS

Each of the Partners covenants for himself or herself, his or her successors and assigns, to execute (with acknowledgment or verification if required) any and all documents and writings which may be reasonably necessary or expedient in the creation of the Partnership and the conduct of the Partnership business. Each of the Partners hereby grants to each of the Managing General Partners, i.e., JOHN JONES and SAM BARKER, a continuing Power of Attorney and Agency (which agency is coupled with an interest) to execute a Certificate of Limited Partnership with respect to this Limited Partnership and to execute under said Power of Attorney and Agency any amendment or cancellation of said Certificate as may be required. It is further acknowledged that execution of any documents on behalf of the Partnership by the Managing General Partners, or either of them, in accordance with the provisions above relating to management shall be binding upon the Partnership and its General Partners.

23. NOTICES

All notices which any partner may desire or be required to give any other partner shall be in writing and shall be given either personally or by prepaid first-class mail directed to the partners' address as shown in the Certificate of Limited Partnership, or as later entered upon the books of the Partnership pursuant to written notification of the General Partners.

24. RECOVERY OF ATTORNEYS' FEES

If the Partnership is a party to an action to enforce any of the terms of this Agreement or of any other contract relating to the Partnership, or an action in any other way pertaining to Partnership affairs or this Agreement, the Partnership or such partner, if it or he prevails, shall be entitled to recover its or his costs, including a reasonable attorneys' fee, incurred in prosecuting or defending the action.

25. EFFECTIVE AGREEMENT

This Agreement shall be binding upon the parties, their respective heirs, assigns, executors, administrators, and successors in interest. Each of the parties acknowledges that he or she has freely entered into this Agreement and without reliance upon any representations expressed or implied by any other party. Each of the parties acknowledges receipt of a confidential memorandum which was prepared prior to the formation of the Partnership by the Managing General Partners. Each of the partners acknowledges notice of the disclaimers contained in said confidential memorandum and acknowledges that such party's participation in this Partnership is based upon such party's independent determination based upon such party's own judgment and the advice of independent advisors and consultants. This Agreement is the entire Agreement between the parties and supersedes any and all other negotiations, correspondence, or discussions between any of the parties.

26. CHOICE OF LAWS

The laws of the State of California shall govern all matters with respect to this Agreement, including all matters relating to formation, construction, and performance of this Agreement.

27. FINDER'S FEE PARTICIPATION OF CERTAIN GENERAL PARTNERS

All of the Partners acknowledge notice that JOHN JONES and SAM BARKER, or either of them, will or may participate in finder's fees or broker or salesman's commissions in connection with the acquisition and/or sale or exchange of real property by the Partnership, and specifically the real property heretofore mentioned in this Partnership Agreement. Each of the Partners hereby consents to such participation and agrees that such fees and/or commissions shall be the property of said Partners, in accordance with agreements between such partners individually and the seller of any such real property.

28. RIGHT OF FIRST REFUSAL

No voluntary or involuntary transfer of any Partnership interest in this Partnership shall be effective unless and until such Partnership interest shall first be offered for sale to the Managing General Partners. In the event of a proposed sale or prospective involuntary transfer, the transferor shall provide to the Managing General Partners written notice of such impending sale or transfer not less than sixty (60) days prior to the proposed effective date of transfer. Each and all of the terms and conditions of such prospective sale or transfer are to be set forth in said notice. Within twenty (20) days after receipt of such written notice the Managing General Partners shall elect to exercise the right of first refusal granted herein or to waive the same. Such election shall be made in writing. On condition that the prospective sale or transfer is a bona fide sale or transfer and that the terms of the same have been accurately disclosed to the Managing General Partners in the aforementioned notice, such waiver of the right of first refusal by the Managing General Partners or the failure of the Managing General Partners to either elect to exercise such right or to waive the same shall be deemed to be a waiver of such right and the proposed or prospective sale or transfer may be completed as contemplated subject to the limitations on transfers of General Partners' interest set forth in Paragraph 18 above. In the event that the Managing General Partners elect to exercise such right of first refusal they shall proceed with the purchase of said interest in accordance with the terms set forth in said notice at the time and in the manner in which said sale or transfer was to originally take place.

GENERAL PROVISIONS

This Agreement may be executed in any number of counterparts, each of which shall be in original, but all of which shall constitute one and the same Agreement.

IN WITNESS WHEREOF, the parties hereto have executed this Agreement this ______ day of __________

GENERAL PARTNERS:

Dated: ______________________ ________________

Dated: ______________________ ________________

Dated: ______________________ ________________

LIMITED PARTNERS: ________________

____

____

____

____

____

* * *

PORTSMOUTHE DEVELOPMENT

c/o Jones Real Estate

2345 Elm Terrace

Los Angeles, California 90049

PARTICIPATION AGREEMENT
PORTSMOUTHE DEVELOPMENT

Adoption

The undersigned hereby specifically accepts and adopts each and every provision of the Certificate and Agreement of Limited Partnership and grants the powers of attorney set forth herein of Portsmouthe Development and acknowledges receipt of a copy thereof.

Participation

The undersigned agrees to purchase a percentage set forth above his/her signature and hereby tenders the amount required to purchase these units.

Representations and Warranties

The undersigned hereby represents and warrants that:

A. He/she is an adult resident or domiciliary of the State of California, and submits the following information as verification of his/her residence:
   (1) I have resided in California since ________ .
   (2) I filed a California resident's income tax return in 1978 ( ) Yes ( ) No, and ( ) have ( ) will file(d) a California resident's return in 1978.
   (3) I am employed ( ) Yes ( ) No. If "Yes", at ________________________________ .
   (4) I am a registered California voter ( ) Yes ( ) No. If not, I am ( ) am not ( ) registered in any other state.
   (5) I own an automobile ( ) Yes ( ) No. If "Yes," it is ( ) is not ( ) registered in California.
   (6) I am employed in the State of California ( ) Yes ( ) No. I am retired ( ) Yes ( ) No.
   (7) I have a driver's license in the State of California ( ) Yes ( ) No.

B. That he/she is purchasing this interest for his, her, or its own account or in a fiduciary capacity for a person or entity which meets all of the applicable requirements (or that of a minor child or ward of such person), with the intention to hold for long-term investment rather than resale.

C. That his/her minimum net worth (excluding home, personal furnishings, and automobiles) is $20,000 or more and his/her income per year is $20,000 or more; or that his/her said net worth regardless of income is $100,000 or more.

D. That he/she has received and has carefully reviewed the Memorandum of Sale and the undersigned understands the speculative nature of the investment and the complex nature of transferring partnership interests. In making an investment in the Partnership, the undersigned represents and warrants that he/she has mature business experience, has relied solely on the aforementioned documents and on an independent investigation.

IN WITNESS WHEREOF, the undersigned has executed this Participation Agreement this ______ day of ________, 1979.

The percentage interest is ______________________ .

The total of monies contributed is ______________ .

1. The Partnership interest is to appear in the following name(s):

2. Title to be shown (circle one): Community Property/ Joint Tenants / Tenants-in-Common / Separate Property
3. Social Security Number(s) or Tax Identification Number: ________________________
4. Residence address: ________________________
5. Mailing address: ________________________

6. Business phone: ______________________
7. Residence phone: ______________________

______________________	______________________
(signature)	(signature)
______________________	______________________
(printed name)	(printed name)

Index